AQA
Poetry
Anthology:
Love and
Relationships

Jo Gracey-Walker

Series Editors:
Sue Bennett and Dave Stockwin

HODDER
EDUCATION
AN HACHETTE UK COMPANY

The Publishers would like to thank the following for permission to reproduce copyright material.

Photo credits
p. 11 TopFoto; **p. 12** TopFoto; **p. 15** plus69/Fotolia; **p. 17** Granger, NYC./ Alamy; **p. 19** Ingram; **p. 22** Emi/Fotolia; **p. 33** TopFoto; **p. 38** NASA; **p. 39** TopFoto; **p. 43** TopFoto; **p. 48** TopFoto

Acknowledgements
pp. 21–24, 97 (no. 6) Bloodaxe Books; **pp. 30–32, 98 (no. 9)** David Higham Associates; **pp. 36–39, 98 (no. 11)** Faber and Faber Ltd; **pp. 44–46, 55, 99 (no. 13)** Owen Sheers c/o Rogers, Coleridge & White Ltd.; **pp. 48–50, 99 (no. 14)** Faber and Faber Ltd; **pp. 87–95** Oxford University Press India © Oxford University Press. All other permissions applied for.

Although every effort has been made to ensure that website addresses are correct at time of going to press, Hodder Education cannot be held responsible for the content of any website mentioned in this book. It is sometimes possible to find a relocated web page by typing in the address of the home page for a website in the URL window of your browser.

Hachette UK's policy is to use papers that are natural, renewable and recyclable products and made from wood grown in sustainable forests. The logging and manufacturing processes are expected to conform to the environmental regulations of the country of origin.

Orders: please contact Bookpoint Ltd, 130 Park Drive, Milton Park, Abingdon, Oxon OX14 4SE. Telephone: (44) 01235 827720. Fax: (44) 01235 400454. Email education@bookpoint.co.uk Lines are open from 9 a.m. to 5 p.m., Monday to Saturday, with a 24-hour message answering service. You can also order through our website: www.hoddereducation.co.uk

ISBN: 978 1 4718 5376 0

© Jo Gracey-Walker, 2016

First published in 2016 by

Hodder Education,

An Hachette UK Company

Carmelite House

50 Victoria Embankment

London EC4Y 0DZ

www.hoddereducation.co.uk

Impression number	10	9	8	7	6	5	4	3	2	1
Year							2019	2018	2017	2016

Cover photo © Marion Wear/123RF.com

Typeset in 11/13pt Univers LT Std 47 Light Condensed by Integra Software Services Pvt. Ltd., Pondicherry, India

Printed in Italy

A catalogue record for this title is available from the British Library.

Contents

Getting the most from this guide

This guide is designed to help you raise your achievement in your examination response to the 'Love and Relationships' poetry cluster in the AQA Anthology (Section B) and to the Unseen poems (Section C). It is intended for you to use throughout your AQA GCSE English literature course. It will help you when you are studying the poems for the first time and also during your revision.

The following features have been used throughout this guide:

Target your thinking

A list of **introductory questions** is provided at the beginning of each chapter to give you a breakdown of the material covered. They target your thinking in order to help you work more efficiently by focusing on the key messages.

Build critical skills

These boxes offer an opportunity to consider some **more challenging questions**. They are designed to encourage deeper thinking, analysis and exploration. Building and practising critical skills in this way will give you a real advantage in the examination.

GRADE *FOCUS*

It is possible to know the poems well and yet still underachieve in the examination if you are unsure what the examiners are looking for. The **GRADE FOCUS** boxes give a clear explanation of how you may be assessed, with an emphasis on the criteria for gaining a Grade 5 and a Grade 8.

REVIEW YOUR LEARNING

At the end of each chapter you will find this section to **test your knowledge**: a series of short, specific questions to ensure you have understood and absorbed the key messages of the chapter. Answers to the 'Review your learning' questions are provided in the final section of the guide (p. 104).

GRADE *BOOSTER*

Read and remember these pieces of helpful **grade-boosting advice**. They provide top tips from experienced teachers and examiners who can advise you on what to do, as well as what *not* to do, in order to maximise your chances of success in the examination.

Key quotation

Key quotations are highlighted for you, so that if you wish you may use them as **supporting evidence** in your examination answers. Further quotations can be found in the 'Top quotations' section on page 96 of the guide.

And love is proved in the letting go.
(Cecil Day Lewis, 'Walking Away', l. 20)

Glossary

The glossary boxes give **explanations of difficult words in the poems**. Technical terms that arise when discussing the poems are marked in bold and explained in the 'Glossary of poetic terms' on page 102.

Studying the Anthology poems

You may find it useful to read sections of this guide when you need them, rather than reading it from start to finish. You will probably want to begin by looking at the cluster of fifteen poems that you need to prepare for the examination, but your needs will be different depending on where you are in your literature course.

You may just want to begin by getting a feel for the poems and the issues they raise, or you may wish to focus on a particular poem or poems that you find especially interesting. Many students enjoy the experience of being able to bring something extra to their classroom lessons in order to be 'a step ahead of the game'. Alternatively, you may have missed a classroom session on a particular poem or feel that you need a clearer explanation of a poem that has puzzled you – and the guide can help with this too.

An initial reading of the section on 'Assessment Objectives and skills' will enable you to make really effective notes in preparation for answering examination questions later. It is crucial that you understand the Assessment Objectives and that you know which ones you are going to be assessed on in the different parts of the examination. The AOs are what examination boards base their mark schemes on and in this section they are broken down and clearly explained.

Revising the poems

The poetry questions are in Section B and Section C of Paper 2. Whether you study the poems in a block of time close to the exam or much earlier in your literature course, you will need to revise thoroughly if you are to achieve the very best grade that you can.

You should first remind yourself of the key content of the poems and consider the effects created by structure and language. You might then look at the 'Assessment Objectives and skills' section to remind yourself of what the examiners are looking for in Section B, and then study carefully the 'Tackling the exams' section for Section B. This section gives you useful information on question format, as well as advice on the examination itself, and practical considerations such as the time available for the question and the Assessment Objectives that apply. There is advice on how to approach the question, writing a quick plan, and the importance of making comparisons.

You will find examples of graded responses in the 'Sample essays' section, with an examiner's comments in the margins, so that you can see clearly how to move towards a Grade 5 and then how to move from a Grade 5 to a Grade 8.

Now that all examinations are 'closed book', the 'Top quotations' section will be an invaluable aid, in that it offers you the opportunity to learn short quotations to support points about key themes in the set poems. As a guide, one quotation is suggested for each poem, with a brief accompanying commentary to help you understand why quotations such as this could prove useful in your response.

Dealing with the Unseen poems

This guide also provides advice on how best to deal with Section C of the examination paper, in which you will face questions on two poems you have not previously studied. You will need to answer both questions so it is important to read the section on the Unseen poems (p. 67) carefully. In this section you will learn how to approach the questions with confidence, as well as how to plan and structure your answers in order to achieve well in the examination. Again, graded sample examination responses exemplifying Grade 5 and Grade 8 responses are provided for both questions. Further examples of paired poems to use for practice are also included on pages 100–101.

And finally…

When writing about poetry in both Section B and Section C, use this guide as a springboard to develop your own ideas. Remember: the examiners are not looking for set responses. You should not read this guide in order to memorise chunks of it, ready to regurgitate in the exam. Identical answers are dull. The examiners hope to reward you for perceptive thought, individual appreciation and varying interpretations. They want to sense that:

- you have engaged with the themes and ideas in the poems
- you have explored the poets' methods with an awareness of the context in which they were writing
- you have been able to make thoughtful comparisons between these ideas and methods
- …and, of course, that you have enjoyed this part of your literature course.

Enjoy referring to the guide, and good luck in your exam.

The table below is designed to help you think about how the time periods for each poem and poet relate to each other. It is arranged in chronological order by the year of the poet's birth. (Note that the poem commentaries in this guide follow the order in the anthology, rather than chronological order.)

Poet	Poem
George Gordon, Lord Byron, 1788–1824	'When We Two Parted', 1816
Percy Bysshe Shelley, 1792–1822	'Love's Philosophy', 1820
Elizabeth Barrett Browning, 1806–61	Sonnet 29 – 'I think of thee!', 1845
Robert Browning, 1812–89	'Porphyria's Lover', 1836
Thomas Hardy, 1840–1928	'Neutral Tones', 1867
Charlotte Mew, 1869–1928	'The Farmer's Bride', 1912
Cecil Day Lewis, 1904–72	'Walking Away', 1962
Charles Causley, 1917–2003	'Eden Rock', 1988
Seamus Heaney, 1939–2013	'Follower', 1966
Carol Ann Duffy, 1955–	'Before You Were Mine', 1993
Maura Dooley,1957–	'Letters From Yorkshire', 2002
Andrew Waterhouse, 1958–2001	'Climbing My Grandfather', 2000
Simon Armitage, 1963–	'Mother, Any Distance', 1993
Daljit Nagra, 1966–	'Singh Song!', 2007
Owen Sheers, 1974–	'Winter Swans', 2005

'When We Two Parted' by Lord Byron

Context

Byron is one of two poets in the 'Love and Relationships' cluster who is classified as a Romantic; the other is Shelley, who was a friend of Byron. Romanticism in literature means something very different from the sense of the word 'romantic' when associated with a love affair. Romanticism was an artistic and intellectual movement, a reaction partly against the rational and logical ideas of the Enlightenment that preceded it and partly against the mechanisation of the Industrial Revolution. The movement emphasised the importance of the emotions.

It is generally agreed that Byron wrote this poem about the end of his relationship with Lady Frances Wedderburn Webster, who was married at the time. By the time 'When We Two Parted' was published she was involved in another affair, this time with the Duke of Wellington. Evidence exists of a draft of this poem with an additional **stanza**, in which Byron refers to 'Fanny', a shortened form of Frances. This stanza, however, is not in the published version of the poem that appears in your Anthology. So, although Byron's biography provides evidence that he is the speaker in the poem and that Lady Frances is the other party, the published poem is deliberately vague. There are no specific details about the relationship: features such as the age or gender of the speaker and the addressee are carefully left unidentified. Pronouns – *I*, *thee* and *they* – are used instead of names.

What happens?

The speaker remembers the distressing break-up of a secret relationship some years earlier, and still feels unable to move on. It presents the lover as cold, which is reflected in the background of the cold morning in which the ending of the relationship took place. This is an example of a language feature called **pathetic fallacy**, where the weather or landscape is used to represent the emotions of a character or characters. The persona now hears others – who don't know that the speaker and the lover had been in a relationship – gossiping about the former partner. It ends with the persona wondering what would happen if they met again, and suggesting that the speaker would respond to the former lover 'With silence and tears' (l. 32).

Structure

On the surface the poem looks quite regular. It is made up of four **octets**, each of which has a full stop at the end of the stanza. This appears to divide the poem into four neat, separate units. So at first it looks as

Build critical skills

Do you think the poem can reveal Byron's feelings about a specific relationship as well as being a general expression of the kinds of feelings people may have when a relationship goes wrong?

Build critical skills

The entire poem has only one **caesura**, in line 23: 'Long, long shall I rue thee'. What do you think are the effects of the lack of caesurae generally, and of the use of a caesura at this point?

if each stanza is dealing with a separate point, which could suggest the speaker has come to terms with the break-up. Byron, however, undermines this neat structure, and ideas that start in one stanza flow over into the next. For example, the first stanza creates the idea of cold, with 'cold, / Colder thy kiss' (ll. 5–6); this spills over into the second stanza with 'Sank chill on my brow' (l. 10). The poem also goes round in a circle, as the end repeats the language of 'years' and 'silence and tears' that was employed in the beginning. So, on the surface, the poem seems neat and controlled, but underneath it is disordered. This may reflect the speaker hiding how upset (s)he is beneath a calm exterior.

You can also find tension between regularity and irregularity in the rhythm made by the pattern of stressed and unstressed syllables. A stressed syllable is one that you say with more emphasis, for example in the word 'blackbird' the syllable 'black' is stressed and 'bird' is unstressed. Byron mostly uses a pattern of two stressed syllables per line, indicated in bold below:

> In **si**lence and **tears**
>
> (l. 2)

He uses a varying number of unstressed syllables, however. Here, there are three unstressed syllables in the line, in line 6 there are only two, whereas in line 17 there are four. The pattern of stresses in line 6 is shown in the key quotation. When you look at this quotation, can you also see how Byron disrupts the pattern by suddenly switching to three stressed syllables in lines 5 and 7?

You might think that this disruption in the pattern shows that the speaker's attempts to restrain his/her emotion have failed – the speaker has tried to keep everything regular, but loses control here.

Key quotation

Pale *grew thy* **cheek** *and* **cold**,

Colder *thy* **kiss**;

Truly *that* **hour** *fore***told**

Sorrow *to* **this**.
(ll. 5–8)

Language and imagery

In the key quotation above, there is an effective example of **consonance**. This is the repetition of the same consonant sound, in this case the hard *k* sound in '**c**old,' '**C**older' and '**k**iss'. You might feel this seems aggressive and cutting. What does this tell you about how the speaker feels at this point? What image does it paint of the lover?

Build critical skills

Many key words in the poem begin with a soft **sibilant** sound: 'silence' (ll. 2,26), 'sever' (l. 4), 'Sorrow' (l. 8), 'Sank' (l. 10), 'shudder' (l. 19), 'secret' (l. 25) and 'spirit' (l. 28). You might feel this seems weak and so reflects the speaker's loss of hope. Look at the sibilant **alliteration** of 'share in its shame' (l. 16). Can you feel a sense of secrecy here? Does it seem sinister? How does this relate to the speaker's feeling that this is dishonourable?

Look out for imagery of death throughout the poem. In the key quotation, the former lover is described as 'pale' and 'cold' (l. 5). This suggests a lack of emotion, but also could suggest (s)he is corpse-like. In line 18 the gossip is described as 'A knell' – this is the slow ring of a bell, as would be used for a funeral. The word 'grieve' (l. 26) also suggests bereavement. It is possible to grieve over any loss, but it is most frequently used to mean a response to a death. So, while Byron never explicitly links the breakdown of the relationship to a death, he repeatedly uses language with connotations of death. What might he be suggesting about the speaker, the former lover and the relationship?

Ideas to consider

Characters in literature are sometimes referred to as 'Byronic heroes'. This is a type of antihero who rebels against rules and society; a man of strong passion, often hiding a melancholy secret. He is considered to be represented by the personality and life of Byron, as well as by the characters he created. Byron, for instance, was notorious during his lifetime for his numerous love affairs. He also rebelled against British society and chose to fight for Greece in its war to gain independence. To what extent do you think these characteristics are represented in the speaker of 'When We Two Parted'?

'Love's Philosophy' by Percy Bysshe Shelley

Context

Shelley is the second poet in the 'Love and Relationships' cluster who is classified as a Romantic (see p. 9). 'Love's Philosophy' demonstrates the Romantic emphasis on the emotions; it also focuses on other key Romantic themes, including nature, beauty and imagination.

> **Build critical skills**
>
> Notice how many lines are in monosyllables. Think about the impression this gives you of the speaker and of the person being addressed. Does it seem sorrowful, angry or both?

▲ Lord Byron, by Thomas Phillips (1813)

GRADE *BOOSTER*

Shelley believed that beauty stimulated moral goodness. Often his poetry presents nature as a source of beauty and inspiration as well as a metaphor for human ingenuity. You might like to deepen your understanding of Shelley's concerns by looking at some of his other poems, such as 'Ode to a Skylark', for examples of this.

▲ 'Wanderer above the Sea of Fog', by Caspar David Friedrich (1818)

The Romantics were interested in nature as also expressing an idea called the sublime – a sense of boundless, awe-inspiring greatness beyond beauty. Mountains are often seen as a source of the sublime in Romantic art: one celebrated example in painting is 'Wanderer above the Sea of Fog' by Caspar David Friedrich (1818). You can see this idea being used in Shelley's imagery: 'the mountains kiss high heaven' (l. 9).

What happens?

The speaker addresses an unnamed individual, persuading him/her to enter into a romantic relationship. Successive images suggest that it is natural and right for individuals to form couples. The gender of neither speaker nor addressee is specified. The imagery of a 'sister-flower' (l. 11) that 'disdain'd its brother' (l. 12), however, might suggest that the speaker is male and the addressee female, and that the addressee has previously rejected the speaker as a lover.

Structure

The form becomes increasingly certain and bold. There is an ABAB rhyme scheme. The first rhyming pair in each stanza, however, uses **half rhyme**, where the words almost, but don't quite, rhyme: 'river' with 'ever' in the first stanza, and 'heaven' with 'forgiven' in the second. Shelley makes this seem unbalanced and disturbing, which can make the reader feel more comfortable as each stanza progresses into full rhyme. This can give the impression that the way to feel safe is to give in to the speaker.

You might like to look at patterns of stressed and unstressed syllables. One thing you could notice is how many of the lines end on an unstressed syllable: in the first stanza all but lines 6 and 8; and in the second stanza the whole of the first half. Some examples are the pairs '**sin**gle' / '**min**gle' (ll. 5,7) and also '**hea**ven' / 'for**giv**en' (ll. 9,11). The effect of this can be to make the end of the line feel weak. In lines 6 and 8 this is changed to a stressed syllable at the end of the line: 'di**vine**' / '**thine**'. This is also done in the second half of the second stanza, with the two rhyming pairs '**earth**' / '**worth**' and '**sea**' / '**me**'. This can feel strong and climactic, as if we are moving from uncertainty to certainty. Just like the move from half rhyme into full rhyme, it can encourage the addressee to submit to the reassurance offered by the speaker.

You could also think about the effects of the repeated use of **enjambment** and the lack of caesurae throughout the poem. One possibility is that these help the poem to feel fluid and smooth, which could make it

---

Glossary

Philosophy: a form of careful investigative thinking or a set of ideas

disdain'd (l. 12): treated with contempt

GRADE *BOOSTER*

Remember, when you make a point about the form of the poem, always to relate it to its effects, and keep it relevant to the question.

seem more affectionate. This links to the argument that everything is connected (see Language and imagery, below).

Language and imagery

The imagery of fluids, with fountains, rivers, the ocean and winds, strengthens Shelley's argument that all things blend into one. This moves towards imagery of the sublime in the second stanza – with mountains, sunlight and moonbeams – so that there is a sense of increasing splendour. These images are interlinked with religious language, such as 'heaven' (l. 3) and 'a law divine' (l. 6), so that rejection of the speaker is presented as a breach of godly as well as natural harmony.

Shelley uses **assonance** of the short vowel *i* at several points in the poem. He often combines this with repetition of the soft consonant *n*, as shown in the key quotation. This creates a gentle, soothing, rhythmic pulse, flowing from one line into the next to reinforce the sense of unity.

In the second stanza we see Shelley repeat 'kiss' and 'clasp' in a symmetrical pattern, so that first 'kiss' appears one line above 'clasp' in lines 9 and 10; then this is reversed, with 'clasp' in line 13 and 'kiss' in line 14. This indicates that two apparent opposites can in fact be harmonious parts of one symmetrical whole. Notice the repetition of the *k* sound here has a different effect to that we found in 'cold,' 'Colder' and 'Kiss' in lines 5–6 of 'When We Two Parted'. There, it sounded harsh and aggressive; here, you might find it sounds clear, clean, neat and fitting.

Ideas to consider

Shelley was expelled from Oxford University after refusing to recant the atheistic views he expressed in a pamphlet called 'The Necessity of Atheism'. How do you think his radical religious ideas at that time sit with his appeal to a divine law in 'Love's Philosophy'?

'Porphyria's Lover' by Robert Browning

Context

Robert Browning, alongside other Victorian poets such as Alfred, Lord Tennyson, is celebrated for developing the **dramatic monologue** – a single narrative voice speaking at a critical moment that is often used to reveal a disturbing personality. You may find it helpful to refer to some of Browning's other dramatic monologues to provide context. In the 'Power and Conflict' section of your Anthology you will find 'My Last Duchess'. This is another poem by Browning and it also presents a man who is frustrated at being unable to control a woman and so chooses that she must die.

Key quotation

***N**oth**ing in** the world **is** s**ing**le*

*All th**ing**s by a law d**i**v**ine***

***In** one another's be**ing** m**ing**le—*

*Why **n**ot I with thi**ne**?* (ll. 5–8)

Build critical skills

You might like to comment on the effect of the shift from short to long vowel assonance at the end of the first stanza. For example, do you think that by slowing the pace it could be seen as more emphatic? Does it show the sadness of the speaker without the beloved?

GRADE BOOSTER

When you are comparing poems, remember that you are looking for differences as well as similarities. An excellent way to do both is to notice when poets use the same technique to different effect.

Build critical skills

Do the three titles alter your impression of the poem and of the speaker? Does the original title's focus on Porphyria rather than on the 'Lover' make a difference? Does the context of the pairing with 'Johannes Agricola' affect your interpretation? Think about the reference to God's silence in the final line.

The poem was first published in 1836 and entitled simply 'Porphyria'; it was republished in 1842 paired with another dramatic monologue, 'Johannes Agricola in Meditation', under the title 'Madhouse Cells'. In 'Johannes Agricola' the speaker expresses his belief that God has already determined that his soul will go to heaven, meaning he is free to sin as much as he likes without punishment. It was not until the 1860s that the poem was renamed 'Porphyria's Lover'.

What happens?

After the narrator's description of a raging storm, Porphyria arrives at his cottage. He is entirely passive while she bustles about, making everything cosy and rearranging the position of his body. Suddenly he springs into activity and strangles her with her own hair. He repositions her corpse in a macabre echo of the way that she had positioned him in the first half of the poem, and for the rest of the night lies with her head on his shoulder.

Structure

Browning uses the form to show that, while the speaker believes he is rational and sane, he is in fact mentally unbalanced, and also to reveal his obsessive, compulsive need for control. He writes in **iambic tetrameter**. This is illustrated with the stressed syllables shown in bold here:

A **sudd**en **thought** of **one** so **pale**

(l. 28)

Browning disrupts this pattern at key points. In line 36, for instance, there are three consecutive stressed syllables at the end of the line:

That **mo**ment **she** was **mine, mine, fair,**

(l. 36)

This could show the strength of the speaker's desire for total control over Porphyria. You might also think about the repetition of 'mine' and how this is emphasised by the consonance with '**mo**ment'. Does this help to make the speaker seem more self-centred?

Another way Browning disrupts the rhythm is by switching around the stressed and unstressed syllables so that sometimes there is a stressed syllable at the start of a line. Notice, for instance, '**On**ly,' at the start of line 50. It comes at a point where the speaker feels really powerful, because he is now controlling Porphyria's body, whereas before she was positioning his. The emphasis this places on the word 'Only' helps convey how much he enjoys this power. It also emphasises the speaker's disturbed mental state, as he identifies the placing of Porphyria's head on his shoulder as the 'Only' difference – failing to point out the most significant change: that Porphyria is now dead.

The poem has an ABABB rhyme scheme. We might interpret this regularity as part of the need of the speaker to control his entire environment. At the same time, you might think that the asymmetry of this rhyme reflects his psychological imbalance and the way this drives him to excess.

Language and imagery

The poem opens with **personification**, whereby things that are not alive are spoken about as if they have human emotions. The wind is shown as on the attack, with the lake and the trees as its victim. It is described as 'sullen' (l. 2) and acting 'for spite' (l. 3), determined to 'vex the lake' (l. 4). At first, it seems as if the weather is a metaphor for the speaker's situation, with himself, like the elm trees and the lake, a victim: 'I listened with heart fit to break' (l. 5). As the poem progresses, though, we learn that he is an unreliable narrator; this is achieved through evidence that the way he sees the world doesn't match reality. For example, we simply cannot accept that, after she was strangled, Porphyria's eyes 'Laughed' (l. 45) or that her head was 'glad' (l. 53). Therefore the reader needs to reconsider the effect created by the personification. The sullen and spiteful character turns out to be the narrator, as shown by the way he behaves throughout the poem. This makes the wind the appropriate metaphor for him, although he sees himself as represented by the lake and the trees.

▲ The wind, determined to 'vex the lake'

Build critical skills

In the commentary on 'When We Two Parted', we looked at the idea of the Byronic hero (p. 11). Do you think that the speaker here sees himself as a Byronic hero?

I found

A thing to do, and all her hair

In one long yellow string I wound

Three times her little throat around,

And strangled her.
(ll. 37–41)

Build critical skills

Porphyria's hair is referred to as 'yellow' three times (ll. 18,20,39). What connotations do you think this has? You might want to think about stereotypical images of beauty and innocence, both now and in Victorian times; or about the juxtaposition of the yellow fire and the storm outside.

One way Browning shows the obsessive character of the speaker is through his fixation upon parts of Porphyria's body, particularly her hair. It is therefore hardly surprising that he chooses her own hair as the murder weapon. The key quotation is the fourth time he refers to her hair. Now, as he assumes control, it is transformed into an object that is not alive – as 'string'. This helps to show how little interest he has in Porphyria as a person. It can also indicate that he is better at interacting with objects than with people. The rhyme of 'thing' with 'string' can suggest his belief that by transforming her hair into 'string' he has dehumanised Porphyria. His casual tone is almost bored as he refers to this simply as 'A thing to do'.

You can compare this to the way that the narrator uses pronouns to dehumanise Porphyria and to control her. During and immediately after the murder, he refers to 'her hair' (l. 38), 'her little throat' (l. 40), 'her lids' (l. 44), 'her cheek' (l. 47) and 'her head' (l. 49). He then begins to talk not about Porphyria but about her head, so that the pronoun changes to 'it':

> So glad it has its utmost will,
>
> That all it scorned at once is fled,
>
> And I, its love, am gained instead!
>
> (ll. 53–55)

This is consistent with the way that he treats her like an object, rather like a doll, which he controls totally.

Ideas to consider

During his lifetime Robert Browning was far less popular than his wife Elizabeth Barrett Browning, but since then the interest in and popularity of his poetry has increased hugely. Why do you think he may have more appeal for modern audiences than for his contemporary Victorian readers?

Sonnet 29 'I think of thee!' by Elizabeth Barrett Browning

Context

Elizabeth Barrett was already a well-respected poet when in 1844 Robert Browning, at that time unsuccessful as a writer, sent her a letter expressing his admiration for her poetry. She had been living for some time as an invalid in intense pain, spending most of her time in one room and seeing few people outside of her immediate family. A friend arranged for Robert to meet Elizabeth. They continued their relationship in secret, writing more than 570 letters to each other over the course of twenty months. Elizabeth feared the disapproval of her father, who wished her to remain unmarried; and her brothers, who saw Robert as a gold-digger. In 1846, despite the family's objections, they married and emigrated to Italy. During their courtship Elizabeth wrote a series of 44 sonnets expressing her feelings for Robert. The series shows the development of these feelings. In the first sonnet she expresses sadness and regret for the 'melancholy years' she has spent as an invalid and is surprised that what finds her now is 'Not Death, but Love.' Some of the early sonnets reveal her fear that this attractive and strong man, six years younger than her, could not truly love her. As the sonnets progress, they become more intense and confident, so that by Sonnet 43 she is able to declare: 'I love thee to the depth and breadth and height / My soul can reach'.

▲ Elizabeth Barrett Browning

What happens?

The speaker develops an extended metaphor, in which the loved one is a palm tree and her thoughts about him are vines growing around it. In his absence, her thoughts about him grow. At first this seems positive, but then the thought-vines grow so thickly that they obscure the tree. She chooses to have not her thoughts of him but his actual presence, and calls upon him as the metaphorical tree to cast down the vines. She ends by saying that when he is there she does not think about him because she is too busy being with him.

Language and imagery

The central images of the tree and the vine growing around it present the speaker's thoughts as being dependent on the beloved. At first, the tone seems positive. The image of 'twine and bud' (l. 1) suggests fresh, delicate, new growth. This is rapidly replaced, however, by the 'straggling green' (l. 4). Here they have become ugly, which is reinforced by the harsh *g* consonance. The vines become parasitic. The poem suggests that the problem is that the speaker is thinking about the lover but is actually alone. The opening word of the poem is 'I' and this is echoed in long vowel *i* assonance throughout the first two lines:

I think of thee! – m**y** thoughts do tw**i**ne and bud

About thee, as w**i**ld v**i**nes, about a tree

(ll. 1–2)

Key quotation

Because, in this deep joy to see and hear thee

And breathe within thy shadow a new air,

I do not think of thee – I am too near thee.
(ll. 12–14)

Build critical skills

What do you think are the effects of keeping the whole poem in the present tense?

Build critical skills

Look at the use of enjambment at the ends of lines 1 and 3. Could this suggest the thought-vines growing out of control? You might like to contrast this with the effect of the enjambment at the end of lines 10 and 12. Do you feel the speaker's excitement here?

This can make it feel like the speaker is an isolated 'I'. By the end of the poem, assonance shifts the focus away from the word 'I' and on to 'thee'. Long vowel *ee* assonance is now used in the key quotation: 'in this d**ee**p joy to s**ee** and hear th**ee** / And br**ea**the' (ll. 12–13). This draws the reader's attention to the word 'thee'. This can help the reader feel the excitement of the difference made when the lover is actually present.

She addresses the lover with imperative verbs: 'Renew' (l. 8), 'Rustle' (l. 9), 'set' (l. 9) and 'let' (l. 10). This might imply that in terms of language she has the power. Yet only he has the strength to tear down the vines that she has created, because he is the one who is physically powerful. This is emphasised by the use of **plosives** in: '**D**rop heavily **d**own, – **b**urst, sha**tt**ered' (l. 11). Combined with the onomatopoeia, these convey his immense energy and the force with which he is able to free himself.

Structure

Barrett Browning makes the poem feel balanced and controlled, expressing how reassuring the speaker finds the lover. As a **Petrarchan sonnet**, the poem begins with a group of eight lines (an octet), and finishes with a group of six lines (a **sestet**). It is typical of this form that she creates a problem in the opening of the octet that is resolved in the sestet. Together with the regular rhyme scheme and use of full rhyme throughout, this generates a feeling of neatness and closure.

Because sonnets are written in **iambic pentameter**, the lines usually have ten syllables with every second syllable stressed, as in: 'I **think** of **thee**! – my **thoughts** do **twine** and **bud**' (l. 1). Barrett Browning uses this to generate a pulse, which is reassuring in its regularity but at the same time enables us to hear the speaker's growing excitement like the beating of a heart. Where she makes subtle alterations to the rhythm, these can convey the intensity of her emotions or the strength of the lover. For example, there is an extra unstressed syllable at the start of line 7 with: 'Who art **dear**er'. This gives additional energy, so that we can hear her excitement. At the beginning of line 9 the stress pattern is reversed, with the first syllable stressed instead of the second: '**Rus**tle'. This expresses the added energy brought by the lover; the way in which he is able at a single stroke to free himself; and the thrill she feels in his actual presence.

The poem also makes effective use of caesurae. The only caesura where the sentence actually comes to an end is in the middle of line 7. On either side of it there are briefer caesurae in the form of commas: 'Who art dearer, better! Rather, instantly'. This is the turning point of the poem, where it moves from thoughts about the lover to a desire for his presence. Do you think the dramatic pause mid-line emphasises the speaker's thrill upon recognising this solution?

Ideas to consider

Notice how much of the language is monosyllabic. What does this suggest about the speaker's feelings or about the nature of the lover? What impact does this have on the way you respond to words that are polysyllabic (not monosyllables)?

'Neutral Tones' by Thomas Hardy

Context

Hardy wrote 'Neutral Tones' in 1867, although it was not published until 1898. While many of his later poems focus on his failed marriage with his first wife Emma or on the happy period of their early relationship, he did not meet Emma until 1870, after this poem was written. 'Neutral Tones' was therefore about a previous relationship, which some have suggested was with his cousin Tryphena Sparks. In 'Neutral Tones', however, Hardy is careful to give no personal details about the woman, so that she cannot be identified. What matters is the failure of the relationship, and her attitude towards him. You might like to compare this with some of the poems about Emma and about Hardy's views of what went wrong in their relationship, such as 'The Going', which was written about Emma's death. At the same time you need to remember that Hardy is creating a persona in the poem: it does not even identify the genders of the parties involved.

The pessimism of 'Neutral Tones' is seen often in Thomas Hardy's writing, not only regarding romantic relationships but also concerning the negative effects of the Industrial Revolution or the Victorian class system. In his novels he is keen to capture an image of the countryside, which he feels is being destroyed by industry. The countryside shapes the lives of those who work the land, helping to form their characters. You might like to compare this with the way that 'Neutral Tones' shows that what is going on in the natural setting reflects the relationship.

What happens?

The speaker looks back to a winter's day when he and his lover stood by a pond. Their relationship is dying so that the lover seems merely bored by him. The poem uses pathetic fallacy, meaning that the death of the couple's feelings for each other is suggested by the depressing winter scene of a white sun and a tree whose fallen leaves have landed on the 'starving' (l. 3) ground around the pond. The final stanza makes clear that the poem is written at a time when the relationship has been long over.

▲ Thomas Hardy

Glossary

chidden (l. 2): told off

sod (l. 3): turf, i.e. grass and the area of soil underneath

curst (l. 15): an alternative spelling for 'cursed'

Structure

Hardy uses the form of his poem to create a stagnant feel. It is cyclical, with the final stanza returning to the images of the first, such as the pond, sun and tree. Each stanza follows an ABBA rhyme scheme, so that they appear to turn in on themselves and prevent progress. This can create the effect of a sense that nothing has been achieved.

Build critical skills

Look at how Hardy uses repetition with a difference. In the first stanza the sun is 'white, as though chidden of God' (l. 2) but by the final stanza it is 'the God-curst sun' (l. 15). You could think about how much stronger 'curst' is than 'chidden'; also how 'as though', which indicates this is just a subjective impression, differs from the certainty of the last stanza.

In the fourth stanza Hardy also uses long vowel assonance to link all four of the final words: 'deceives', 'me', 'tree' and 'leaves'. Do you think that this sounds like it is grinding to a slow, painful halt? The second stanza is similar, with repetition of the long vowel *o* in 'rove', 'ago' and 'fro'. You might also like to comment on the rhyming pair 'rove' and 'love' in this stanza. Although they use the same spelling, they do not sound the same. One interpretation would be that 'love' is the word that seems most out of place in the poem.

Language and imagery

In place of the passionate excitement of a violent break-up, the couple is worn down into neutrality. Hardy keeps the language deliberately simple and repetitive. Six of the sixteen lines begin with the word 'And'. Look at how often Hardy uses the indefinite article 'a', rather than the definite article 'the', to describe the background scene: 'a pond' (l. 1), 'a few leaves' (l. 3), 'an ash' (l. 4) and 'a tree' (l. 15). This can help to express that there is nothing special about them. You might think this suggests the couple is so out of love that it just isn't worth the effort to think about it that clearly.

Hardy uses the sounds of the words throughout to give a listless tone. In the first stanza, the alliteration of *w* in 'was white' following upon 'We' and 'winter' in the first line helps to create a tired, bored mood. This is reinforced by alliteration of further soft sounds in 'leaves lay' (l. 3), 'starving sod' (l. 3) and 'fallen from' (l. 4). The colour imagery develops this as Hardy takes objects that are normally associated with vibrant colours and brings them within his neutral palette, the yellow sun becoming white and the green leaves becoming first grey and then the even vaguer 'grayish' (l. 16).

The former lover's smile is presented paradoxically in this key quotation. The smile is personified but is given life only for it to die. The use of 'deadest' is also confusing, since it is not possible for one thing to be *more* dead than another. Hardy uses enjambment so that the structure of the poem makes a pause where there is not one in the sentence. This means that when we reach this pause at the end of one line there appears the certainty that the smile is already dead, only for the next line to reverse this and show that it is instead dying.

Key quotation

The smile on your mouth was the deadest thing

Alive enough to have strength to die
(ll. 9–10)

Ideas to consider

Hardy was famous for his rejection of Christianity. Why do you think he chooses to rhyme 'God' with 'sod' (meaning a piece of earth) in the first stanza? How does this relate to the shift from 'chidden of God' to the stronger 'God-curst' in the final stanza? Do you think that Hardy is passing comment on the concept of a loving god? Alternatively, is it designed rather to tell us about the state of mind of the speaker?

Build critical skills

Hardy also uses long vowel i assonance in 'smile', 'Alive' and 'die' in the key quotation so that the three words key to this paradox become linked. You might feel that you can hear the word 'I' echoed here. If so, do you think the speaker is hinting at the selfishness of the lover? Alternatively, you may feel the repetition of a long vowel sound accentuates the sense of pain experienced.

'Letters from Yorkshire' by Maura Dooley

Context

Maura Dooley spent some time working in Yorkshire prior to moving to London, so this poem might draw upon personal experience. One key theme is the power of writing. You might like to relate this to the poet's professional life, which is dedicated both to her own writing and to assisting others to express themselves through writing. She is the author both of prose and several poetry anthologies, such as *Sound Barrier* in which 'Letters from Yorkshire' first appeared in 2002. In 2014 she became the Poet-in-Residence at the Jane Austen's House Museum. She teaches creative writing at Goldsmiths, University of London, and on residential courses for the Arvon Foundation. She founded and directed the Literature programme at the Southbank Centre in London, and has been a judge for several writing competitions, such as the T. S. Eliot Prize and the National Poetry Competition.

What happens?

A man planting potatoes sees the return of the first lapwings (a ground-nesting bird found usually on farmland), so goes indoors to write a letter to the speaker, whose gender is not specified. The effects of the man's outdoor work are seen positively: although his knuckles are 'reddened' (l. 4) by moving to the warmth of indoors, they are described as 'singing' (l. 3).

▲ A lapwing

The narrator states: 'It's not romance, simply how things are' (l. 5). You might decide that 'It' refers to the relationship between the man and the speaker, and therefore this indicates that it is a friendship rather than a romantic relationship. Alternatively, 'It' may refer to the description of the man, which would present him as very down-to-earth, or to the content of the man's letter, which would therefore be presented as plain and honest. With either of these latter interpretations, it would still be possible to see this as a romantic relationship.

The speaker juxtaposes the man's life, with its outdoor work, against the narrator's, typing on a computer, and asks whether the man's is 'more real' (l. 9). The narrator suggests that he would not think that. The poem, however, shows that the man belongs in both the outdoor world and the interior world of creative writing. He not only has direct contact with the outdoors, but actively communicates through the act of writing the letter. Just as outdoors he is 'clearing a path through snow' (l. 11), so his writing clears a way for the speaker to return mentally to Yorkshire. The poem ends with an image conveying that, although they are living in different houses and miles apart, they are linked because they are watching the same news on TV.

Structure

The poem uses **free verse** to create a fluid structure. Although there are three lines to a stanza, the lack of end rhyme and the frequent use of enjambment prevent rigidity. Just as the man in Yorkshire and the speaker can communicate with each other despite the physical distance, the separation into stanzas does not restrain the flow of ideas and language. The effect of the enjambment is particularly clear between stanzas, as here it picks out points of transition or contrast. Between stanzas 2 and 3 the enjambment of 'knuckles singing / as they reddened' (ll. 3–4) highlights the effect of moving indoors from the cold outside, from physical labour and observation of nature to the process of writing.

The natural background, by talking about seasonal change, can remind us that in one way time goes around in a circle, always returning to the same time of year. You could look at how enjambment is used to highlight this between the second and third stanzas: 'seasons / turning' (ll. 6–7). As one stanza turns into another, the language draws our attention to the way that seasons take us back to where we were.

Between the fourth and fifth stanzas the enjambment draws attention to the power of language to recreate the writer's world for the speaker, as illustrated by the key quotation. This begins and ends with the only caesurae made by a full stop in the poem, which gives it additional prominence. The enjambment helps to slow the pace of the sentence. This is reinforced by the additional caesura one syllable into the sentence, and

Build critical skills

Two points in the poem run counter to this use of enjambment. Lines 5 and 9 are each a single, complete sentence, so that the sentence exactly matches the line. What do you think are the effects of this in each instance?

by the soft, soothing sibilant **s** sounds and assonance of the short vowel *i*: '**s**now. **St**i*ll*, *it'***s**'. The word 'you' is emphasised since the enjambment places it at the end of the line, and because it rhymes with the first word of the next line: 'who'. Then, as the poem moves into the next stanza, the **metaphor** of 'pouring air and light' is used, as the poem literally pours from one stanza into the next.

Although end rhyme is avoided, the poem uses internal rhyme and the echoing of sounds. You might notice the repetition of 'see' in line 6 with '*see*ing the *se*asons', which is then continued in a more fragmented way two lines later with 'scr*ee*n'. Within this eighth line, *ee* is not only the last vowel sound (in 'scr*ee*n'), but also the first (in 'f*ee*ding'), so that the end of the line returns to the beginning. Which of the characters sees the seasons and which sees a screen? What kind of feeding, metaphorical and literal, is done in the processes of gardening and writing?

Key quotation

Still, it's you

who sends me word of that other world

pouring air and light into an envelope.
(ll. 11–13)

Build critical skills

Look at the use of the homophone pair 'sow'/'so': 'sow' as the final word of the rhetorical question in line 9; and 'so' in the man's supposed answer in line 10. These sounds are then picked up in line 11 with 'snow', line 13 with the repetition of 'So' and line 15 with 'souls'. How does this link seasonal change, renewal, the value of physical labour, relationships and the power of language?

Language and imagery

The poem compares different media for communication. The man uses the more traditional method of the letter, while the speaker types at a screen. Both watch the news on television. This enables the creative process of gardening to be linked to that of writing. The words 'planting' and 'sow' reflect how the man is involved in the creation of life. The personification of 'feeding words onto a blank screen' links the production of writing to that of the plants growing in the garden, as the screen too needs to be fed. The man's activity of 'clearing a path through snow' (l. 11) reflects the way that writing metaphorically clears a path for information and ideas to pass. Every part of him is communicative, even his knuckles are personified as 'singing'.

You could also look at the way that the poem uses the sound of words. The opening line is rich with plosives: '*digging* his *garden*, *planting potatoes*,' so that we can hear the tools against the ground, and feel the man's energy. The alliteration of '*planting potatoes*' and the assonance of '*digging his*' give a neatness, symmetry and lightness. Do you think these help to show how the speaker sees the man's activities positively?

Build critical skills

Compare this with the use of sibilance in the final line: 'our **s**oul**s** tap out me**ss**age**s** acro**ss** the i**c**y mile**s**.' This combines with the alliteration of '*messages*' and '*miles*' and the long vowel assonance of 'icy miles'. You might feel that this creates a wistful, longing tone of regret at the distance between them. Alternatively, you could decide that this is soothing and therefore reassuring because, despite that distance, they are still able to communicate.

Ideas to consider

In the first stanza, the man is referred to using the pronoun 'he'; by the second stanza he has become 'You'. It is not until the final stanza that the first person plural is used, with 'our souls' as they watch 'the same news'. How does this affect the reader's understanding of the relationship?

'The Farmer's Bride' by Charlotte Mew

Context

Charlotte Mew demonstrated a strong interest in mental health issues, not only in 'The Farmer's Bride' but also in her other works of both poetry and prose. Her own life was an inspiration for this concern: two of her siblings were committed to mental institutions at a young age; and it is reported that she and her sister vowed to remain childless as they believed that this was hereditary.

Equality for women is another issue highlighted by this poem, and Mew's life is relevant again here. She contravened her society's expectations of appropriately demure feminine behaviour by dressing in tailored suits in the style of a man and by travelling to France without an escort. You might like to think about the suffragette movement to demand votes for women as symbolic of the fight for female equality at this time. Mew lived from 1869 to 1928 and, although this poem was written in the nineteenth century, it was published in 1912. The first MP to call for women to be allowed to vote was John Stuart Mill in 1866 and the vote was granted first in 1918 to a limited group of women over the age of 30; it was not until 1928 that it was granted to all women over 21.

What happens?

A farmer recounts the story of his three-year-long marriage. He tells that his wife, afraid of both him and other men, runs away. Together with members of his community, he brings her back and locks her in. Now, as Christmas approaches, he regrets that there are no children in the house. By the end, he appears to be driven to desperation by his desire for her.

Structure

Mew plays with the tension between regularity and irregularity to show the stress experienced by the farmer and the bride. Both the rhyme and rhythm vary throughout the poem, but within sections they create a pattern that leads the reader to expect it to continue – an expectation that can then be frustrated. Many of the lines are written in iambic tetrameter. This includes the first four lines, for example: 'At **har**vest-**time**

GRADE *BOOSTER*

It will help you develop your ideas about context if you think about ways in which a poem's contemporary audience might have reacted similarly to or differently from a modern audience.

Glossary

maid (l. 1): an unmarried girl or woman, usually indicating a virgin

woo (l. 3): to seek the affections of a woman, normally with a view to marriage

fay (l. 8): fairy

leveret (l. 30): a young hare, less than one year old

rime (l. 38): frost

than **bide** and **woo**'. This enables Mew to make the reader feel uncomfortable when she then breaks this pattern. Lines 5 and 7, for example, add an additional unstressed syllable at the end: 'things **hum**an;' and 'a **wom**an'. The half rhyme of 'human' and 'woman' reinforces this disturbing effect.

The second stanza is again dominated by iambic tetrameter, but dramatically alters when the community pursues the bride, employing a line double this length: 'So **ov**er **se**ven-**a**cre **field** and **up**-a**long** a**cross** the **down**'. We therefore hear the energy and effort of the chase as well as the exhaustion of the hunted bride.

The poem is a dramatic monologue, so that we hear only the farmer's point of view. We therefore are left to infer the bride's outlook. Yet we never feel that we have managed to understand her side of the story because the farmer is an unreliable narrator and we have no other source of data. By acknowledging that 'more's to do / At harvest-time than bide and woo' (ll. 2–3), he shows how little he has got to know her and how he does not even see why this should be important. His assertion that 'she turned afraid' (l. 4) after their marriage indicates that her fear is inexplicable to him and groundless; he does not even stop to consider whether he bears any responsibility for this. So the reader's only source of information about the bride cannot be depended upon.

It is part of the sensitivity of the poem, though, that Mew is able to show how he oppresses the bride and yet at the same time to invite empathy for him. He is ignorant rather than malicious, bewildered as to why she does not meet his expectations. It is possible both to be horrified at how close he comes to being overcome by his sexual desire and yet to sympathise with the way he is being torn apart by this. This can be seen most clearly in the final stanza:

> Alone, poor maid. 'Tis but a stair
>
> Betwixt us.

(ll. 42–43)

He seems to pity her by referring to her as 'poor maid'. From this point of view, his observation that she is 'Alone', which Mew emphasises by placing this word at the start of the line and isolating it from the remainder by a caesura, would seem to indicate pathos for her. Yet at the same time, the repetition of the word 'maid', used at the start of the poem, reflects his frustration that, despite all that has intervened, she remains a virgin. With this in mind, the emphasis on the word 'Alone' takes on a darker interpretation, that he sees how defenceless she is – how easily he could force her into intercourse. The enjambment supports his perception that there is nothing but a stair between them: the word 'stair' hangs at the end of the line, like part of an actual staircase, showing

Build critical skills

Look at the length of the lines in the fifth stanza. Why do you think many of them are drawn out? How does this relate to the ideas of time passing?

Build critical skills

Do you feel that our empathy with the farmer and the bride remains constant throughout the poem? Alternatively, do you think there are points when our sympathy for the one increases as it decreases for the other?

how easy it is to progress from one stair to the next. The sentence is at once two things and one, because it is a single sentence but split over two lines. This can be interpreted in a way sympathetic to the farmer as it reflects his inability to comprehend why the two of them should remain separated. At the same time it reveals the damage caused by his ignorance, because placing the word 'stair' at the end of the line highlights that he thinks this is the only thing separating them: he fails to see the contribution of his own attitudes and behaviour. Moreover, it emphasises to the reader the threat to the bride should he fail to restrain himself.

Mew, in this final stanza, uses a rapid succession of caesurae – a total of nine in the final four lines of the poem – to reveal the intensity of the farmer's emotion. This is particularly strong with the repetition of exclamation marks in line 44. Again we can interpret this as the farmer suffering as he struggles to restrain himself, and simultaneously as revealing the menace he represents to the bride as he seems increasingly unable to do so. These caesurae are part of the way his **syntax** breaks down. The final sentence is grammatically incomplete since it lacks a verb. The farmer descends into incoherence as he cannot phrase a complete idea, but simply lists the physical features that have become the object of his obsession: 'her eyes, her hair, her hair!' The repetition stresses the alliteration of *h*, so that we hear him panting.

Language and imagery

The absence of the word *wife* is remarkable: she is referred to not only as a 'maid', implying that she remains a virgin, but as a 'bride' – a term used to refer to a woman on, or close to, her wedding day. This strengthens the idea that there has been no positive development in the relationship between the farmer and his bride since their wedding: there has effectively been a wedding but no marriage. This contrasts with the language of time that permeates the poem. The first stanza draws upon the semantic field of seasonal change: 'Three Summers since', 'At harvest-time', 'a winter's day' and 'in the Fall'. This reflects the farmer's familiarity with the seasons and the expectation he derives from his profession that he should gain from the passing of time. In the fourth stanza he focuses on the descent into winter. This operates as pathetic fallacy, reflecting his despair. It also presents negative images of winter as indicating the death of the year. Colours are used to emphasise the coldness and starkness of winter, with the 'blue smoke' (l. 35), 'grey sky' (l. 35) and 'black earth spread white with rime' (l. 38). These are juxtaposed against the positive anticipation of Christmas. The berries not only are red, but 'redden' (l. 39), indicating progress. Despite the bleak background, they are able to ripen. Yet this means nothing to the farmer without children. So there is a sense that time ought to bring progress, but where there is no development towards a goal, the result is merely decay.

The farmer's proximity to nature is likewise reflected in the animal imagery he uses to describe the bride. His **similes** of the hare and the mouse are importantly of animals that have not been domesticated and that are prey, reflecting both his frustration that she eludes his control and his predatory instincts towards her. The leveret, a hare less than one year, also serves to stress how young she is. You might want to consider why the farmer picks the leveret as a simile for the bride, then specifies its gender as masculine with 'he'. This is one of three similes in the fourth stanza. The other two, comparing her to 'a young larch tree' and to 'the first wild violets' similarly reflect her youth, fragility and existence outside of the elements of nature that he controls through farming.

By comparing her also to 'a fay' (l. 8), he shows how little he understands her: her rejection of his advances makes him feel that she is not only inhuman in the way that a wild animal is, but that she moves into the realm of the mythical. In this way he blames his failure to relate to her entirely upon her by claiming that she belongs to a world beyond human understanding.

Mew is celebrated for her ability to capture the regional dialect of the farmer and his community, illustrated by the key quotation. One contemporary admirer of this was Thomas Hardy.

The dialect gives the quotation an immediacy and realism. The simplicity of the vocabulary and the use of monosyllables in all words other than 'away' combine to show how limited the farmer's understanding is of the complex situation. Notice also the emphasis on times of both the day and the year. This is the only line in the poem that is exactly one sentence long, because both it and the preceding line are **end-stopped**. These work together to express the intensity of the bride's misery and the perplexity of the farmer, while creating a dramatic pause.

Ideas to consider

What role do you think the community plays in the poem? Are you able to infer anything about the attitudes of other women towards the bride?

'Walking Away' by Cecil Day Lewis

Context

Cecil Day Lewis published this poem in 1962, although it was written in 1956. It was dedicated to his son Sean. The final stanza opens with 'I have had worse partings,' and so you may wish to relate it to the context of Day Lewis' turbulent personal life. During the 1940s, while married to Sean's mother, he was having an affair with the author Rosamond Lehmann, and dividing his time between living with Lehmann and trips

---

Build critical skills

Notice the strong use of sibilance in the fourth stanza, such as '**Sh**y a**s** a leveret, **s**wift a**s** he'. Do you think the seems soft and fragile, reflecting the precarious position of the bride; seductive, illustrating the farmer's attraction towards her; sinister, hinting at the threat he poses to her; or all three?

Key quotation

One night, in the Fall, she runned away.
(l. 9)

Glossary

pathos (l. 8): something that generates pity or sadness

fledged (l. 8): describes a young bird with feathers that are able to support flight

gait (l. 9): the way a person walks

eddy (l. 11): move in a circular way

irresolute (l. 15): uncertain

back to his family home. Then, in 1950, he left both his first wife and Lehmann to marry the actress Jill Balcon. Their children were born in 1953 and 1957. The poem was therefore written at a time when Day Lewis had started a second family, but is looking back to a point eighteen years earlier, before he had met Lehmann. These autobiographical details aren't included in the poem itself, however, and, as always, a persona is created for the speaker; the gender of neither parent and nor child is identified.

You could also relate the sentiment that 'love is proved in the letting go' (l. 20) to Day Lewis' feelings about his own childhood. Following his mother's death from cancer in 1908, his father became intensely over-protective of him, showing what he later termed 'smother love'. He came to see boarding school as an escape from this.

What happens?

A parent recalls a day eighteen years earlier, when his child played a football game at school for the first time. The persona focuses on the moment when the child is walking away from him. This becomes symbolic for the change in their relationship, as the child is growing up and the parent has to let him become free. The speaker begins by expressing great anxiety about this, but steadily moves towards acceptance. He finally links this to a reference to God: you might choose to infer that this is the Christian God, who showed love by giving Jesus to the world. This enables the parent to conclude that independence is necessary for selfhood and that love is proved by letting the loved one go.

Structure

The poem has a regular structure, with four stanzas, each of which has five lines following an ABACA rhyme scheme. You might find this feels reassuring: that, although the speaker feels anxiety and pain, all takes place within the support of the parent's love for the child and the love of God referred to in the final stanza. Alternatively, you might like to suggest it shows that the son's instinct to seek independence is relentless, driving strongly forward despite the effect it has on the parent.

Yet the poem draws our attention away from this regularity by the frequent use of enjambment and caesurae. Look at the first sentence as an example. It has so many sub-clauses that it becomes extremely long and spills over into the second stanza. This can give the sense of the huge jumble of emotions felt by the speaker. This leads into the caesura ending the sentence in line 6. Once the son disappears 'Behind a scatter of boys', this flow of thought is brought to an abrupt close. It is as if the speaker has been cut off from the child.

Most of the lines start with an unstressed syllable, for example 'A **sunny day**' (l. 2) or 'And **love** is **proved**' (l. 20). There are, though, points where this is

GRADE *BOOSTER*

Looking out for a range of effects for a single technique can help you uncover alternative readings.

reversed, so that the line starts instead with a stressed syllable; we see this for instance in '**Wrenched** from' (l. 5). To show the intense pain of the son being pulled away, the persona surprises the reader by using enjambment to place this forceful, stressed monosyllable at the start of the line.

Language and imagery

The development of the speaker's thoughts is shown through a succession of different images. We begin with subtle suggestions that this is a time of transition: 'with leaves just turning, / The touch-lines new ruled' (ll. 2–3). The autumn leaves are beautiful, yet they foreshadow the death of the year; in the same way, just as it is a pleasure for the parent to see the son's developing skills as he plays football, they foreshadow the death of the son's dependence on the parent. You might also feel the 'touch-lines' (l. 3) function as a metaphor for the changing limits in the intimacy of parent and child. For example, is an older child less comfortable about being hugged by a parent in front of their peers?

Each of the first three stanzas offers a simile to illustrate the child leaving the parent, and the progress from one to the next suggests that the parent is becoming gradually reconciled to this. The first, of 'a satellite / Wrenched from its orbit' (ll. 4–5), seems unnatural. The definition of a satellite is something that orbits a planet, so that without the planet it actually ceases to be a satellite. Day Lewis also uses short vowel assonance '*i*ts orb*i*t, go dr*i*fting' (l. 5). This can give a sense of pointless wandering. Does the speaker feel that without his support the child has no purpose and direction? How does this work together with the emphasis placed on the disturbing word 'wrenched'?

The next simile focuses on the parent's fear that without his support the child will be in danger: 'With the pathos of a half-fledged thing set free / Into a wilderness' (ll. 8–9). This seems part of a more natural process: there comes a time when birds must leave the parents' nest. The threat here, though, is that the departure seems premature, since it is only a 'half-fledged thing', so is not yet sufficiently mature for flight.

The third simile shows much more acceptance that this is natural: 'eddying away / Like a winged seed loosened from its parent stem' (ll. 11–12). The imagery has progressed from the harsh 'wrenched' to 'eddying away' and 'loosened', which seem gentle and fluid. It benefits both the offspring and the parent plant for seeds to be dispersed away.

Finally, the speaker is able to reach acceptance in the key quotation. The idea of 'walking away' has finally taken on a positive meaning for the speaker. The child is not only leaving the parent but is gaining selfhood. The parent is not merely passively left behind but is actively proving his love. You might like to look at how this is given a gentle mood by the consonance of the soft *w* sound in 'Ho**w** selfhood begins **w**ith a **w**alking a**w**ay' (l. 19).

Build critical skills

What effect does the repetition of the word 'away' have on you? Does it make a difference whether it is at the end of a line – or of a stanza? Three times (if we include the title) it is preceded by 'walking' (ll. 7,19); once by 'drifting' (l. 5); once by 'eddying' (l. 11). Does this make it feel different?

Build critical skills

Think about the effect that some of the more unusual language choices have on you. Why do you think the poet personifies the parting with the word 'Gnaws' in line 17? What impression do you have from the use of 'scatter' as a collective noun in 'a scatter of boys' (line 6)?

Key quotation

How selfhood begins
with a walking away,

And love is proved in
the letting go.
(ll. 19–20)

Ideas to consider

The references to time relate both to seasonal change and to the passing of years. Looking back over eighteen years, the parent recalls a boy who at that time was a child but now is an adult. Look at how tenses are used, such as 'I watched' (l. 3) and 'I can see' (l. 6). Does the speaker feel as if he is addressing the adult or the child? How vivid is the memory in the speaker's mind?

'Eden Rock' by Charles Causley

Context

Charles Causley spent most of his life in Launceston, Cornwall, where he grew up. After service in World War II, he completed teacher training and returned to work at the local primary school, where he taught until retirement. His father died when he was only seven, as a result of a lung condition contracted fighting in the trenches of World War I. Close to his mother, he remained unmarried, and nursed her at home for the last six years of her life after she had a stroke. He was buried in Launceston alongside his mother.

In other poetry, Causley recalls childhood memories of his father. You might like to look at 'To My Father' as part of the context for 'Eden Rock'. In 'To My Father' he recalls his last image of him before his death: 'Possessed by fearful coughing. Beats the floor / With his ash stick,' but also remembers him as an 'Immaculate young countryman, his mouth / Twitching with laughter.' You might relate this to the carefree, strong image in 'Eden Rock' of 'My father spins / A stone along the water' (ll. 15–16). You could also link the beckoning of the parents to the speaker in 'Eden Rock' with the ending of 'To My Father': 'I know that one day he must stop and turn / His face to me. Wait for me, father. Wait.'

What happens?

The speaker describes his parents in an idyllic picture of domestic family life. His father's pet dog is by his feet, while his mother prepares a picnic. The speaker is on the other side of a stream from his parents. His father skims a stone and then his parents beckon him across the stream, encouraging him by telling him that it is easier to cross than he thinks.

Some people have interpreted this poem as looking towards the speaker's own death: his parents have already made the crossing into the world beyond death and wait for him to join them, calming his fears. Others have suggested that it depicts a time before the speaker's birth, so that his parents are inviting him to join them in life. You can also see it as a vivid memory, coloured by nostalgia for the past; it is moving because the

> **Glossary**
>
> **tweed (l. 3):** a thick, woollen cloth
>
> **sprigged (l. 5):** a pattern of small bunches of flowers, often used for dress material

> **Key** quotation
>
> *I hear them call, 'See where the stream-path is!*
>
> *Crossing is not as hard as you might think.'*
> (ll. 18–19)

more perfect it is in the speaker's mind, the more he must regret that he can never recover that past. It also can be seen as being about the nature of parent–child relationships: this one experience can be a metaphor for all the times that the speaker's parents helped him to develop through their encouragement. Think about the ways in which parents are able to assist their children to take on new skills, because they themselves have already developed them, such as learning to kick a football or ride a bike. Of course it is possible to see the poem as all these things at once. It is part of Causley's skill that it can evoke each of these ideas without excluding others.

Structure

The first four stanzas are all four lines long; this creates a pattern that is then broken by a three-line stanza and a concluding single-line stanza. The earlier regularity can encourage us to feel that this ought to be one four-line stanza but that it has been fragmented, and to want to pull that last line into the other three. This supports the idea of the parents beckoning the child, to unite himself with them on the other side of the stream.

The first three stanzas all contain enjambment within the stanza, but each of them finishes with an end-stopped line. Do you think that this matches the neat, idyllic images? This pattern is disrupted with the enjambment between the fourth and fifth stanzas: 'Leisurely, / They beckon to me'. This can help the reader feel the draw of the parents, as the fifth stanza is pulled into the fourth by the continuation of the sentence. At the same time, the division between the stanzas can act as a reminder of the stream that divides the parents from the child. It is preceded by the only two caesurae made by the ending of sentences in the poem: 'My father spins / A stone along the water.' This helps to slow the pace prior to the enjambment, to enhance the soothing and reassuring tone. Do you think it also makes us think about crossing dividing lines?

The structure makes the transition from the third to the fourth stanza pivotal. Throughout, half rhyme is used in an ABAB pattern, as in the pairings 'dress' / 'grass' and 'hat' / 'light' in the second stanza. The only full rhyme is in the third stanza's second and last lines: 'screw' / 'blue'. This can alert the reader to a moment of drama. Interestingly, Causley chooses to focus this on the homely image of milk and cups, consistent with his elevation of his parents' most ordinary activities to a grand status. It also creates a pause, thus preparing the way for transition from the realism used up to this point into the more bizarre image that opens the next stanza: 'The sky whitens as if lit by three suns.' You might also notice the focus that it places on colour.

> **Build critical skills**
>
> What is the effect for you of the end-stopping that is used for the last four lines?

> **Build critical skills**
>
> What do you think is the effect of using half rhyme for most of the poem? Do you find that you notice the half rhyme as you read, or is it more subtle?

Language and imagery

The scene is recalled in loving detail: the exact ages of not only the parents but also the dog; the fabric of the parents' clothing; the choice of 'an old H.P. Sauce bottle' (l. 10). Look at how the description of the father in line 2 and the mother in line 5 exactly mirror each other. One interpretation is that this emphasises their similarity and provides harmony. Colour is used to make this more vivid, such as the mother's hair in line 8 being 'the colour of wheat'. This can make her seem wholesome and also as if she naturally blends in with the landscape as an integral part of it, an impression reinforced as it 'takes on the light' (l. 8).

Build critical skills

You might like to explore the similarity between the word 'wheat' used for the colour of the mother's hair and 'white' used to describe the cloth in the previous line. White then rhymes with 'light' at the end of line 8. This helps link her hair to the ideas of both white and light, each of which has connotations of purity and both of which are associated with many representations of heaven.

You might consider that the title 'Eden Rock' has subtle overtones of Christian imagery. The Garden of Eden, as presented in the Book of Genesis of the Bible, is the paradise on Earth that Adam and Eve forfeit by eating the fruit from the tree of the knowledge of good and evil. In the New Testament (Matthew 16:18) Jesus, speaking to Peter, states: 'upon this rock I will build my church'. You might choose to see the title as evoking ideas of a lost paradise on Earth, of man's redemption through Jesus and of the paradise of heaven. You may therefore feel that 'The sky whitens as if lit by three suns' (l. 13) has connotations of the three souls of the parents and the speaker, and also of the Christian concept of the Trinity, whereby the one God has three persons: the Father, the Son and the Holy Spirit.

Build critical skills

Look at the use of tenses throughout the poem. It is written mainly in the present tense. However, in line 7 the mother 'has spread' the cloth and in the final line the speaker reflects: 'I had not thought'. How does the use of the present tense make the poem feel? What effect do these exceptions have on your interpretation of the poem?

Ideas to consider

The final line is deliberately ambiguous: 'I had not thought that it would be like this.' It does not specify what 'it' and 'this' are. Is the speaker looking back with regret at that perfect time, and thinking that he did not think then that his later life would have turned out as it did? Is he thinking that before birth he could not have realised how wonderful life could be? Is it that this image has changed his conception of death?

'Follower' by Seamus Heaney

Context

Seamus Heaney grew up on his father's farm in Northern Ireland, although he later lived in the Republic of Ireland. Among many other awards, he received the Nobel Prize for Literature in 1995. The depth of his understanding of the English language and its history can be seen not only in his poetry but also in his translations, such as his prize-winning translation of *Beowulf* from Old English.

'Follower' was published in 1966 in the anthology *Death of a Naturalist*. It is typical of the poems of this collection in dealing with childhood memories, life in the countryside, family relationships and the process of growing up. It is often compared to 'Digging', from the same anthology. This draws upon images of Heaney's father digging potatoes and his grandfather cutting turf; it suggests that although he admires them, he cannot match their standards in working the land: 'But I've no spade to follow men like them.' Instead he has his pen and so 'I'll dig with it.' You might like to relate this to the speaker's desire to 'grow up and plough' (l. 17) in 'Follower'.

> **Glossary**
>
> **furrow (l. 3):** a long, narrow trench made by a plough in a field
>
> **wing (l. 5):** part of the plough
>
> **sock (l. 6):** the part of the plough blade that cuts the soil
>
> **sod (l. 7):** turf, grass and the area of soil underneath
>
> **headrig (l. 8):** the point in the field where the horse and plough have to turn around

▲ A horse-drawn plough

What happens?

The speaker recalls his father as an expert ploughman using the traditional horse-drawn method, describing the details of how he prepares and then sets out to plough. He expresses total admiration and a desire to be like his father, but sees himself as a nuisance as he follows him around. In the final stanza there is a surprising shift: the poem moves into the present and shows the father, now older, as 'stumbling / Behind me', suggesting the inevitable reversal of their positions.

Structure

The poem is written in **quatrain** (four-line) stanzas, with what could at first appear to be a regular ABAB rhyme scheme. There is a pattern, however, of one rhyming pair using full rhyme and the other using half rhyme. In the first stanza, for example, 'strung' / 'tongue' is full rhyme but 'plough' / 'furrow' is half rhyme. You might feel that this reflects the regular rising-and-falling motion of the plough. Alternatively, you may consider that it reflects the speaker's perception that his father was perfect but his child self failed to live up to the father's standard.

The final stanza breaks the pattern. The pair 'today' / 'away' rhymes; with 'falling' and 'stumbling', the final syllable is identical. One way to interpret this would be to see the speaker as reaching adulthood and so feeling that he is now strong. Another would be that the rising and falling of the plough has now come to an end in the father's old age.

The predominant rhythm is iambic tetrameter. You can see this in: 'An **expert. He** would **set** the **wing**' (l. 5). This is frequently altered, however, and many lines start on a stressed syllable. An example is '**Yapp**ing' (l. 22), where we feel the child self of the speaker to be intrusive. Another is '**Narr**owed' (l. 11), followed by '**Mapp**ing' in the next line, where the precision of the father's expertise is conveyed. Caesurae are used powerfully, for instance in line 5 the father is termed simply 'An expert.' The caesura indicates the father's perfection: no further explanation need be offered because the father's status is beyond dispute.

In the final stanza, the caesura emphasises the sudden shift from the past to the present: 'Yapping always. But today'. The enjambment then helps to emphasise the word 'today' by placing it at the end of a line. Enjambment is used further in 'stumbling / behind' to indicate the change in the relative positions of father and son. It is as if the father literally stumbles off the end of the line and falls into the new circumstance of being the 'Follower'.

This compares interestingly with the way that enjambment is used in the key quotation (p. 35). Here, contrasting with the sense of stumbling in the final stanza,

GRADE *BOOSTER*

Look for rhyming patterns and then also ways in which these are broken, focusing on the effects of this.

Build critical skills

Look at the caesura and notice also how the enjambment emphasises the word 'eye' in line 10. What effects do you think these have?

we see the masterful control of the father ploughing. We make a transition into the next stanza, just as the horses must make a transition by turning. Then, as the horses 'turned round', so too does the sentence, as it turns into the next line.

Language and imagery

This key quotation also highlights two central features of the poem's language. First, it uses the technical terminology of farming without comment or effort, to show that not only the father but also the speaker have been immersed in this world. Second, it creates imagery through the sounds of words. Look at the consonance in 'swea**t**ing **t**eam **t**urned' (l. 9). This both emphasises the regularity of the movements and recreates the sounds of the plough. The softness of the short vowel assonance, as in 'head*ri*g, w*i*th a s*i*ngle' (l. 8) and 'A*n*d ba*ck* into the la*n*d' (l. 10), conveys that the horses have such respect for the father that they obey with only the gentlest guidance.

Imagery is used to emphasise the father's power and expertise. Central is the nautical imagery, which compares him and the act of ploughing to a ship sailing. The simile of the first stanza takes the image of the father's shoulders curved as he works and elevates this to the magnificence of a sailing ship: 'shoulders globed like a full sail strung' (l. 2). The long vowel assonance in 'sh*ou*lders gl*o*bed' can give a sense of effortless strength. The sailing ship, like the horse plough, precedes the days of mechanisation; the fullness of its sails indicates that it proceeds at full power with the assistance of nothing but the wind. The verb 'globed' emphasises this splendour, with connotations of his father being the whole world. He is as strong as Atlas, who in classical mythology supports the Earth; or a ship that circumnavigates the whole planet. The nautical imagery continues with: 'The sod rolled over without breaking' (l. 7). A wave can roll, meaning it continues in a fluid movement, or it can break, when it collapses. This not only stresses the father's intense skills, it also conveys his apparently ceaseless energy. It captures the child's boundless admiration, but in turn makes the final stanza's image of the father 'stumbling' more disturbing. In line 13, the noun 'wake' connotes the trail of water left by the passage of a ship. This conveys how enormous the impression left by the father is, but also shows that for the son it is like attempting to sail in disturbed water, so that it is at once more difficult to follow and to choose his own path.

Ideas to consider

The final words of the poem – 'will not go away' – could seem suddenly harsh, as if the speaker is tired of the father. Alternatively, they could suggest that despite any difficulties in the relationship, the father remains there for the son. Do they have any other meanings for you?

Key quotation

At the headrig, with a single pluck

Of reins, the sweating team turned round

And back into the land. (ll. 8–10)

Build critical skills

There are a number of followers in the poem. The father follows the plough; the horses follow the commands of the father; the child follows the father; later the father follows the son. The speaker wishes to become like his father. Think about all the connotations that the word 'follower' generates and about how the different concepts relate to or exist in tension with one another.

'Mother, Any Distance' by Simon Armitage

Context

This poem was first published in 1993 in *Book of Matches*. Each of the poems in the collection is based on the **sonnet** form and is designed to take the same time to be read out loud as it takes for a match to burn.

Simon Armitage is now a full-time writer who has achieved success in a range of prose forms, including drama as well as poetry. He was appointed Professor of Poetry at the University of Sheffield in 1991 and at the University of Oxford in 2015. At the time *Book of Matches* was published, he was working as a probation officer in Manchester.

The topic of growing up and seeking independence is one you can find elsewhere in Armitage's poetry. You may like to look at 'Kid', which explores the idea of needing to break free from an older role model through Batman's sidekick Robin. You might also want briefly to refer to how other poets have treated the same issue of parents and children both being dependent on each other and wanting individual freedom, such as 'Catrin' by Gillian Clarke. Like Armitage, Clarke uses the umbilical cord to symbolise the relationship. Both of these poems have appeared on the AQA syllabus in the past, so copies of them are widely available.

Statistics indicate that the age to which children remain in their parents' home has increased dramatically in recent years. According to the Office for National Statistics, the percentage of 20–34-year-olds living with their parents rose from 21 per cent in 1996 to 26 per cent (32 per cent for men) in 2013. This means that in 2013, 3.3 million in this age group were still living at home. You might feel this reflects a change in attitudes. Alternatively you might feel that the tension between dependence and the need for self-determination has always existed, but that changing economic circumstances have placed it under even more pressure since the poem was written. Do you think this social change would make a difference to how readers respond to the poem, or are the basic longings people experience the same?

> **GRADE BOOSTER**
>
> Remember that context can include relating a poem to the specific social and historical circumstances in which it was written, but can also mean recognising ways in which it pushes beyond a particular moment to convey universal issues and values.

What happens?

The narrator, whose gender is not specified, needs the mother's help to measure a new home in order to furnish it. As the tape measure unwinds, it becomes an extended metaphor for their relationship. The mother remains on the ground floor of the house, while the speaker, tape measure in hand, moves upwards, until the tape measure reaches 'breaking point' (l. 10) at the entrance to the loft. The narrator nevertheless continues to move even further away. At the end the speaker reaches for independence – presented as 'an endless sky' (l. 14) – with it remaining unanswered whether this will lead to success or failure: 'to fall or fly' (l. 15).

Structure

The poem is broadly based on the sonnet but it is the way that it deviates from this that is most revealing about the speaker and the relationship. In addition to the traditional fourteen lines, there is a short fifteenth line; this could reflect the speaker reaching forwards into the future. It might suggest that the narrator has taken too great a risk in overstepping boundaries, or that (s)he has finally attained freedom. You might also find it interesting to look at the ellipsis in the final stanza: 'the last one-hundredth of an inch...I reach'. It is 'inch' and not 'reach' that rhymes with the 'pinch' of the previous line. This can make it feel as though the line should end there, and therefore that 'I reach' is pushing beyond boundaries. So you might feel a tension between the positive interpretation of escaping limitations and the negative one of going too far and into danger.

The rhyme pattern starts with two quatrains (blocks of four lines). In the first quatrain, the rhyming couplet of 'doors' / 'floors' is balanced against the half rhyme of 'span' / 'hands'. This could indicate the narrator's feeling that in some ways the relationship with the mother is desirable and appropriate, but that in other ways (s)he wants to reach beyond its confines. In the following quatrain three successive lines end in -*ing*: 'recording', 'leaving' and 'unreeling'. This might indicate moving towards greater neatness, reflecting the safety offered by the mother's presence; alternatively the use of repetition could suggest that the mother's presence is increasingly stifling. This pattern is suddenly reversed in line 8, which does not rhyme with any of the previous lines: 'Kite'.

This makes line 8 a pivotal turning point in the poem, which Armitage emphasises through his structure. You might notice that enjambment is used throughout the second quatrain: do you think this reflects the tape measure unwinding? It is gentle and fluid, which can suggest a tender relationship. Suddenly there are two single-word sentence fragments; and so there are two caesurae made by full stops within line 8. This focuses attention in on those two important metaphors but also disrupts the steady flow of the extending tape measure. You might like to view this as reflecting underlying tension within the relationship, or as the child hesitating to move any further away at this point.

Language and imagery

The extended metaphor of the tape measure forms the focus of the poem. The ambiguity of 'feeding out' could imply simply that it is becoming longer, but also suggests the umbilical cord. The necessity of the connection between the mother and the child is further conveyed by the image of 'space-walk' (l. 9): one way to keep an astronaut close to the spacecraft in minimal gravity and at the same time provide a supply of air is to use a connecting tube known as an umbilical cable. The thrill of space exploration was originally

Key quotation

the line still feeding out, unreeling

Years between us. Anchor. Kite.
(ll. 7–8)

Build critical skills

The poem is a dramatic monologue, addressed entirely to the mother. Is it possible for us to know the mother as well as the speaker, or does the dramatic monologue form prevent this? After all, we know only what the speaker chooses or is able to tell us about the mother, and the speaker cannot see into the mother's mind.

possible only because of the security provided by the cable. You might like to relate this to the context. The first astronaut to fly free in space without an umbilical cable connecting him to the space shuttle was Bruce McCandless in 1984, meaning that by the time this poem was written the umbilical cable was still used but was no longer necessary. You might see this as part of the way the poem shows that we can become less dependent over time.

▲ An astronaut on a space walk with an umbilical cable

There is a paradoxical sense that the speaker can only become independent of the mother because she provides the support that gives the speaker the confidence to try things alone. The earlier language of 'reporting metres, centimetres back to base' (l. 6) can suggest that the narrator can progress only because (s)he is linked to a secure base. The alliteration of the firm sounding *b* helps to give this a sense of a stable foundation. You might also feel that it gives it a rule-based, regimented, military feel, which conflicts with the narrator's drive towards freedom.

The mother is described as 'at the zero end' (l. 5). Literally, this is because she is holding the stationary end of the tape measure. It also links into the language of space travel, with the mother part of the base at the countdown. In positive terms, it draws attention to the way that the mother has been a continuing presence since the narrator's birth. It also has negative connotations, however, suggesting how little significance she now has in the speaker's life. This relates to 'unreeling / years between us' (ll. 7–8). There are years between them because they have spent so many years together, yet also because the generation gap forms a barrier.

The pivotal point of 'Anchor. Kite.' (l. 8) draws upon this idea of a connecting cable. An anchor provides an essential function to a ship, in preventing it from drifting, which is dependent on the cable. Yet if it malfunctions — if the anchor becomes stuck when the ship tries to raise it — it impedes the ship's movement. The kite floats freely, just as the speaker desires to do, but only functions as a kite if it is attached to a string that is held at ground level: otherwise it flies out of control.

Ideas to consider

The poem is far from static, so the speaker's feelings towards the mother develop as it progresses. Think about how the language and structure change. Are there points where the speaker needs to know that the mother is securely there in order that (s)he can have the freedom to explore? Are there points where the narrator feels the need to break away entirely? Is the speaker perhaps unsure which of these (s)he wants? Has the speaker come to a decision about this by the end?

'Before You Were Mine' by Carol Ann Duffy

Context

Carol Ann Duffy was appointed Britain's first female, and first Scottish, Poet Laureate in 2009; 'Before You Were Mine' was originally published in *Mean Time* in 1993. Although we need always to be careful to look at how poets create a persona for the voice of the poem, Duffy makes it clear that this poem is autobiographical through the precise details of proper nouns such as George Square. Therefore referring to brief autobiographical details can be relevant to context. Duffy lived with her Roman Catholic family in Glasgow until the age of six, when they moved to Stafford in England. With four younger brothers, she was the eldest child.

You might find it helpful to look at 'Brothers', another poem that takes a nostalgic look at Duffy's family relationships and explores how they are affected by the passing of time. Her mother appears in the poem as the individual who named the brothers: 'I like to repeat the names. / My mother chose them.'

'Before You Were Mine' also refers to popular culture, such as the name 'Marilyn'. Marilyn Monroe in many ways personified the glamour of 1950s Hollywood. The image in the poem of the polka-dot dress blowing around the mother's legs evokes two iconic photographs: one entitled 'Seaside Chat' by Bert Hardy; the other of Marilyn Monroe in the 1955 film *The Seven Year Itch*, standing above a subway grating that blows up her dress.

▲ Marilyn Monroe in *The Seven Year Itch*

39

This indicates the mother has given up that glamour through the act of motherhood, suggesting this is a loss to her. You might feel, however, that it also reveals what the mother has gained. Marilyn Monroe suffered several miscarriages, so motherhood might be seen as gaining something that was denied to Monroe. In *The Seven Year Itch* she plays a single young woman whose neighbour fantasises about leaving his wife and son for her, but he comes to his senses and at the end of the film sets off to find his family. So on the one hand the image endorses the glamour of the sexually attractive young female, but more subtly it can reinforce the value of motherhood and so the choice her mother made. At the same time, the mother's status in the child's eyes is revealed by the association of her with this epitome of glamour and stardom.

Build critical skills

Both the first and the last names of the mother's friends are given: 'Maggie McGeeney and Jean Duff' (l. 2). Yet Marilyn Monroe is so famous that all of these ideas can be conveyed by her first name only. What does this indicate about whether the narrator ever actually met (so as to become on first-name terms with) the friends from her mother's youth? Does it make any suggestions about the value of celebrity?

What happens?

The narrator pictures her mother as a young woman, prior to her own birth. She presents an image of her laughing with her friends, attending dances to meet young men, and getting in trouble with her own mother for returning home late. She recalls herself as a child, placing her hands in her mother's red shoes, and remembers how her mother taught her the Cuban dance the cha-cha as they returned from mass. The whole poem is infused with a sense of paradox: she longs to know her mother as the young woman she was before she took on the responsibilities of looking after her children – but she cannot possibly do this because it was her own birth that brought about the change.

Structure

The poem avoids a regular rhyme scheme, but shows regularity in that each of its four stanzas is five lines long and is end-stopped. Some readers have suggested that this makes it look like photographs regularly spaced out in an album. You might feel it represents the compartmentalisation of the mother's life into different phases, before and after children; the constancy of the love that mother and daughter feel for each other; or the relentless progress of time. Enjambment helps to give a conversational, informal tone; it could also show the unity of the three friends in the opening stanza. In line 2 it stresses the word 'with' by placing it at the start of the line. In lines 3-4 they are 'holding / each other'. By placing 'holding' on one line and 'each other' on the next, while the sentence continues to flow, it is as if line 3 reaches out to hold on to line 4.

One of the ways that the poem plays with the idea of time is through the tense of its verbs. As you read, you could note how often the present tense is used. The effect is most noticeable when the speaker uses the present tense to talk about herself during the period ten years before her own birth. You could look at the opening of the second stanza: 'I'm not here yet.' – this is as self-contradictory as replying 'Absent' when a register is called. On the one hand, this is Duffy projecting herself back in time; but on the other, it is bringing the mother's past self into Duffy's present. The monosyllabic, simple sentence ending can present the simplicity and purity of the child's longing for the mother. It might, though, be read with a sense of warning or menace – the word 'yet' foreshadowing the change that is to come.

This tense alters in the final stanza, so that now the past tense is used: 'I wanted' and 'before I was born.' With 'I wanted' the speaker is talking about the history and constancy of her own feelings for the mother, rather than about the mother herself. There is an important change in tone between 'Before you were mine' and 'before I was born'. The latter, but not the former, acknowledges that there was a time when the narrator did not exist. You could also consider the way that the past tense is used in the third stanza, in line 11, with the word 'was'. The use of the past tense, then, is associated with the absence of something desired: the daughter failing to gain direct access to the younger self of the mother; the daughter not yet existing; the irretrievable loss of the mother's freedom.

Language and imagery

At times the narrator appears to accuse herself of restricting her mother's freedom by demanding her attention. This is reflected in the language. Although it is essentially a love poem, so that we might expect it to be focused on the mother, first person singular pronouns (*I, mine, my, me*) are used frequently. They are foregrounded by being placed in prominent positions. Look at the first and last words of the poem and the first word of the second stanza. Enjambment is used to place 'I' at the start of line 18. You can link this to words such as 'possessive' in line 11 as well as to the demanding 'I wanted' in line 18. Notice how this is balanced against the use of second person pronouns (*you, your*). Do you think that this focuses on the relationship between the mother and daughter, or does it emphasise that they are separate? When you are thinking about this, you should bear in mind that there are no first person plural pronouns (*we, us, our*) in the poem.

> **GRADE BOOSTER**
>
> Look out for ways in which poets create patterns and then go on to break them. Explore the effect of both the pattern and its disruption.

> **Build critical skills**
>
> The language is kept accessible and often colloquial. Look at 'pals' (l. 2), 'Ma' (l. 9), 'hiding' (l. 10) and 'reckon' (l. 10). Carol Ann Duffy has said that, rather than using complicated language, she likes to use simple language in complex ways. How do you think she achieves that here?

The language carefully stresses the glamour of the mother. You might like to explore the consonance used in the repeated *l* sound of 'That glamorous love lasts / where you sparkle and waltz and laugh' (ll. 19–20). Its soft fluidity expresses the narrator's admiration and love for her. The idea of this endurance through time coexists with images that suggest this self is in the irretrievable past.

Key quotation

I remember my hands in those high-heeled red shoes, relics,

and now your ghost clatters towards me over George Square

till I see you, clear as scent
(ll. 12–14)

This can also be seen by looking at the key quotation. The red shoes are referred to as 'relics'. This implies a remnant of a very distant past, but also has religious connotations. In faiths such as Catholicism the physical remains of saints are often preserved as relics and treasured with veneration. It therefore suggests that the shoes belong to a time that has passed, but that they continue to exert enormous power over the present through their enduring value. The word 'ghost' likewise conveys that this past self is no longer alive, but that it continues to haunt the present. You might like to relate this to ideas about the use of tenses discussed in the section above on 'Structure'.

The key quotation also helps us to look at sensory imagery in the poem. Much of the poem builds on visual imagery, as is consistent with the primary means of access to the mother's younger self being through photographs. In this quote, though, we have the sound imagery of the onomatopoeic 'clatters'. In 'I see you, clear as scent' there is a deliberate confusion of sight and smell. The image is so lifted out of mere photographs into the imagination that it is as if the mother is really present and so can be smelt. Do you feel that this blending of senses is continued in line 15 with the internal rhyme of the visual 'lights' and the tactile 'bites'?

Ideas to consider

There is a circularity to the poem. The final words are identical to the title. The word 'laugh' appears in both the first and last lines. Both the opening and closing stanzas show the mother on a pavement. Yet here there is a key difference: the carefree laughter is replaced with attending to her daughter's needs as she returns from mass. What do you think the poem means by 'stamping stars from the wrong pavement' (l. 17)? There would be a literal way in which their shoes would make a stamping sound, because it was common at this time to attach small metal studs to the heels and toes of shoes to make them last longer. Do you think this could also be a reference to the stars on Hollywood Boulevard (the Hollywood Walk of Fame)? If so, does it suggest that the mother ought to have been a Hollywood star? Would this imply that becoming a mother prevented her from personal achievements? Or does it rather convey the extent of the daughter's love for the mother that she invests her with this celebrity status?

'Winter Swans' by Owen Sheers

Context

In 'Winter Swans' a couple has relationship difficulties but is encouraged to overcome these by seeing swans while walking around a lake. This way of showing the landscape inspiring people to handle everyday difficulties is frequently found in Sheers' poetry and also in the work he has done looking at other poets. For example, he wrote and presented a TV series called *A Poet's Guide to Britain*, with an accompanying anthology, in which he looked at how different poems show poets responding to landscape.

Although Sheers was born in Fiji, he was brought up in South Wales, and the landscape of that area plays an important part in much of his poetry. 'Winter Swans' first appeared in his anthology *Skirrid Hill* in 2005. 'Skirrid' is the English version of a Welsh word meaning divorce or separation, as well as shake or tremble. There is a hill in Wales called Skirrid Hill, or Skirrid Fawr, which is owned by the National Trust. It has a broken shape caused by a huge landslide, and there is a legend that this was caused by either an earthquake or a lightning strike at the same time Jesus was crucified.

▲ Skirrid Fawr

A unifying theme of the poems in that collection is fractured relationships and the environments in which they exist. You might therefore find that other poems from *Skirrid Hill* form an interesting part of the context for 'Winter Swans'. The poem 'Farther', for example, explores the legend that the broken shape of Skirrid Hill was caused by God's grief at Jesus' crucifixion. In 'Mametz Wood' Sheers examines the idea of separation through a very sympathetic account of the soldiers of the 38th Welsh Division who died taking Mametz Wood in World War I. He introduces the landscape in that poem as a character that needs to be healed of its wounds. You might like to compare this to the way that the personified earth is 'gulping for breath' (l. 5) in 'Winter Swans'.

What happens?

It has been raining for two days but now there is a break in the rain, so a couple go for a walk around a lake. They appear not to be getting on as they are 'silent and apart' (l. 6). Then they stop to look at swans who arrive, dip their heads under the water and then fly away. The idea that the swans 'mate for life' (l. 13) seems to make the couple want to patch things up, as they now hold hands. At the end of the poem it is not made clear whether this is enough to provide a permanent reconciliation or is just a temporary fix.

Structure

One of the first things you might spot about the structure is the length of the stanzas: each is a triplet (three lines) except for the last, which is a couplet (two lines). The couplet could represent the two people becoming united by the end; here an additional line would represent something intruding between them. Alternatively you might feel that the final stanza is missing a line, and so shows that there is something wrong: they have decided to stop arguing but haven't resolved their differences or dealt with the underlying issues.

Another conspicuous feature is the absence of rhyme at the end of the lines. You should, though, be able to find some rhyming patterns; an excellent example is the fourth stanza, shown in the key quotation. The first and last lines of this stanza are linked by half rhyme: 'water' / 'weather'. Within the middle line the words 'white feather' are emphasised by being placed not at the end but instead immediately before a caesura. Because 'white' starts with the same sound as 'weather' and then 'feather' rhymes with it, this can feel like an echo. You might decide this shows that the swans bring a greater unity to the poem. On the other hand you could argue that, by offering us something that almost rhymes, the poem makes us crave the neatness of full rhyme. This may suggest that the couple lacks the harmony of the swans, or that the reconciliation between them prompted by this vision is only superficial.

Build critical skills

Do you feel these interpretations exclude each other, or does the poem suggest both at once?

Key quotation

they halved themselves in the dark water,

icebergs of white feather, paused before returning again

like boats righting in rough weather.
(ll. 10–12)

You might feel that the tension between these interpretations reflects the tension within the relationship, because the couple's longing for unity makes them frustrated when they cannot achieve this.

Enjambment also figures prominently. The first sentence doesn't finish until the end of line 8. This can reflect the enduring nature of not only the couple's dispute but also of their willingness to seek a resolution. The layering of successive sub-clauses within a single, elongated sentence can make the reader long for closure, just as the couple needs to bring their argument to a close. It is therefore significant that the last word in the sentence is 'unison', as this could indicate that the way the couple can find the longed-for closure and harmony is by uniting.

> ### Build critical skills
>
> Another interesting use of enjambment is in the sentence that runs from midway through line 14 to the end. Does this work like the opening sentence, or do you think there is a more fluid, harmonious, reconciliatory feel here? You might feel the sibilance in the sixth stanza affects the mood.

There is only one place where a caesura is used at the end of a sentence, in the fifth stanza: 'porcelain over the stilling water. I didn't reply'. Notice that, prior to this stanza, only the first person plural (*we, us, our*) has been used to describe the couple. In this stanza for the first time the second person singular (*you*) and first person singular (*I*) are used. The fact that they are on separate lines and in separate sentences is emphasised because the caesura comes immediately before the word 'I'. You might feel this suggests that the couple must assert their needs as individuals before they can work together as a couple. Alternatively, you may prefer to see it as indicating the fundamental differences driving the couple apart. This is also the only time that direct speech is used in the poem. The key statement through which the swans inspire the couple is 'They mate for life' (l. 13). Importantly, these are not the words of the speaker, so the other party to the relationship is given a voice in the poem and uses it to express this idea.

Language and imagery

Dense imagery is at the heart of this poem; the ways in which the literal and metaphorical levels interrelate, however, is extremely complex. There is no simple one-to-one correspondence whereby we can say something like *swans equal happy relationship*. We can see from the key quotation above that within the space of a single stanza the metaphor of 'icebergs' and the simile of 'boats righting' are used for the swans. This might suggest a whole range of different ideas. Do you feel that 'icebergs'

> ### Build critical skills
>
> You might also want to pick out the echo of the word 'and' in '*and sand,* / I noticed our *hands, that had*' (ll. 16–17), as well as the similarity in the sounds of 'hands' and 'had'. How do you think this affects the mood?

> ### Build critical skills
>
> How significant do you think it is that the speaker, who has control of the language of the poem overall, had no words to respond to this at the time: 'I didn't reply' (l. 14)?

Build critical skills

Investigate the final image, of the couple's hands coming together 'like a pair of wings settling after flight' (l. 20). In line 18, the hands 'swum', as if each was a separate swan, but now they are transformed into the two wings of a single swan. How does this fit with the theme of division and unity that runs through the poem?

evoke a sense of the sublime (see the discussion of the sublime in 'Love's Philosophy' on p. 12), and that this indicates nature's power to lift the couple out of the more mundane aspects of their existence? Do the icebergs represent the natural world, while the boats represent mankind's skills, instinct to explore and interaction with nature? Or do you find that the combination of these two images offers connotations of a collision, such as that of the *Titanic*? Could the menace that an iceberg presents to a boat imply that the couple's relationship contains the source of its own destruction? If so, what is the significance of the boats 'righting' themselves rather than sinking? How does the image of a huge, rigid and inanimate iceberg fit with the idea of a 'white feather' (l. 11) – small, flexible and part of the living swan? In the next stanza the metaphor used instead is 'porcelain' (l. 14). This draws further attention to the purity of the white colour juxtaposed against 'the dark water' (l. 10). Like the design of the boat, porcelain represents the creativity, ingenuity and inventiveness of mankind. Yet there is also a sense of its fragility.

One interesting example of alliteration is within lines 3 and 4: 'in *w*hich *we w*alked / the *w*aterlogged earth'. You might feel that the soft tone this generates indicates the calm of the environment after the storm. Alternatively this may suggest to you the difficulty the couple have in walking on the rain-soaked ground, which you could view as a metaphor for their struggle to return to friendly terms.

You could also investigate assonance, such as that used in line 8: 'w*i*th a show of t*i*pping in un*i*son'. Because this is short vowel assonance, it helps make the swans seem light and delicate. It also unites the line, and so can reinforce the appeal of union.

Ideas to consider

Think about the opening line: 'The clouds had given their all—'. By using this as a metaphor for the couple's argument, does Sheers suggest that their dispute has been necessary to clear the air? Consider what we mean by the word 'given' in the phrase 'given their all'. You might think that it has more of a sense of doing one's best than of being generous, and can include trying one's hardest to be destructive as well as creative. There is also a specific sense of what it means for a cloud to give its all, because a cloud is destroyed as the water droplets out of which it is composed turn into rain. What does this indicate about what the couple might be doing to themselves by arguing?

'Singh Song!' by Daljit Nagra

Context

Daljit Nagra's parents emigrated in the 1950s from the Indian part of the Punjab to Britain, where he was born in 1966. He writes with great sensitivity about the experiences both of first generation immigrants and of their children born in Britain, and what it feels like to be regarded as both British and Indian. This topic pervades his collection *Look We Have Coming to Dover!*, in which 'Singh Song!' was first published. He is careful to give a dignity to the ordinary experiences of working class people as he explores their search for a sense of whom they are within competing cultures and languages. Ways in which he does this include writing an Indian pronunciation into his poetry, as in 'Singh Song!', or by capturing the grammar of those whose native language is Punjabi, as in the title of the collection. Another way is by showing a blending – sometimes a clash – of cultural influences. The bride in 'Singh Song!' in her tartan sari is typical of the diverse cultural references within the collection – on the one hand an early *Coronation Street* character (Hilda Ogden) and on the other the 1972 Bollywood film *Pakeezah*.

He uses his poetry to work against negative stereotypes by giving individuals, such as the shopkeeper in 'Singh Song!', a voice. You might also like to look at 'Parade's End' from the same collection: the increasing prosperity of a family of Indian shopkeepers is symbolised by their Granada car with its champagne gold paint, which is then vandalised with acid.

The title 'Singh Song!' invites the reader to think about the importance of the name Singh, which derives from the Sanskrit word for lion, in Sikhism. Many Indian surnames can indicate a class or caste. One of the gurus who formed the foundations for Sikhism said that all Sikh males should have the name of Singh, thus forming the idea of a single brotherhood and removing a concept of caste. You might like to relate this to the fact that Nagra's early poetry was written under the pseudonym Khan Singh Kumar. Khan is a widespread Islamic surname; Kumar is a Hindu name that is not specific to any caste. What do you think Nagra could be saying about racial and religious equality by use of this name? Another poem from *Look We Have Coming to Dover!* is called 'Booking Khan Singh Kumar'. This poem uses humour to explore how audiences may expect an Asian British writer to express himself.

Daljit Nagra often performs his poetry and you should be able to find on the internet videos of him reading the poems mentioned here.

> **Glossary**
>
> **chapatti (l. 6):** a type of Indian bread
>
> **plantain (l. 14):** similar to a banana, but larger and savoury
>
> **donkey jacket (l. 33):** a buttoned jacket that has been seen as typical clothing of a male British manual labourer

What happens?

The recently married narrator runs a shop owned by his father but takes every opportunity to close the shop and slip upstairs to his bride. The shoppers complain about the quality of the produce and the service. His wife challenges stereotypes as she is exceptionally modern in her dress, her attitudes and her use of the internet to run a Sikh dating website.

Once the shoppers have left, the couple sit together inside the shop. Their conversation suggests that, unlike everything else in the shop, the narrator's feelings for his bride are something that cannot be sold: 'Is priceless baby–' (l. 58).

Language and imagery

The poem is written in the particular idiolect of the narrator. An idiolect is the distinctive language of an individual; sometimes it can feel like a private language. One aspect of this is non-standard grammar, as seen in 'ven yoo shoppers are wrap up quiet' (l. 44). Another strategy is the minimal punctuation. Notice that, although there are question marks, there is not a single full stop: most frequently a dash is used where a full stop would be expected, for example at the end of the poem. A third feature is the spelling of words to indicate the speaker's accent, such as 'Ven I return vid' in line 10.

One way in which Nagra both explores the relationship between cultures and breaks down prejudice is through the origin of words. The narrator and his bride look out 'at di beaches ov di UK in di brightey moon' (l. 48). The word 'brightey' might appear at first to be merely a grammatical error; it also suggests, however, the informal term 'Blighty'. This word, commonly used by British soldiers during the two world wars to refer to Britain, is an anglicised form of the Urdu word *bilāyatī*, meaning 'foreigner'. So the speaker has given an English word an Indian twist; but this word recalls one that entered the language by giving an English turn to an Indian word. It derives from the presence of the English as foreigners on Indian soil; this word therefore questions the whole idea of what it means to be foreign. You might feel this suggests that, rather than one culture dominating another, each can enrich the other.

One way in which the humour works is by surprising the reader, particularly in the presentation of the bride. The poem sounds like it is about to use a cliché, such as all the colours of the rainbow, but then instead offers: 'she effing at my mum / in all di colours of Punjabi' (ll. 23–24). Notice that the bride is willing to use swear words that her husband will not repeat, but that he instead replaces with 'effing'.

You could also explore the incongruous imagery in the key quotation (p. 49). The opening 'tiny eyes' seems at first to suggest the stereotype of the demure Asian wife, but is instantly transformed by the gun metaphor. This is juxtaposed against the child-like innocence of 'teddy', reinforced by the childish language 'tummy'. These two words are linked by both rhyme and alliteration to develop a nursery rhyme feel. The wife is an enigma, to whom only the narrator has access. Do you think that this makes her seem powerful?

▲ Daljit Nagra

Structure

An interesting structural feature is the way that voices other than the narrator's are included. The poem is a monologue that includes the speech of 'di shoppers' (ll. 11, 36) and of 'my bride' (ll. 22, 27, 30, 35), yet the boundary between direct and indirect speech is blurred. In direct speech, the exact words of the person who spoke them are used within speech marks; in indirect speech there are no speech marks and the narrator can put the gist of what was said into his own words. In 'Singh Song!' the speaker's words are in italics to indicate that they are separate from the words of the shopkeeper, but the absence of speech marks means we cannot be sure that these are their exact words.

Build critical skills

This way of presenting speech means that in one way Singh's bride is given a voice to express herself, but in another she is not because we cannot be sure if these are her words or her husband's. How does this relate to the absence of a female voice through the male narrator in poems such as 'Porphyria's Lover' and 'The Farmer's Bride'?

This is complicated by the way that the other characters' speech is presented in the narrator's idiolect, for example 'Hey Singh, ver yoo bin?' (ll. 12, 37). We do not know if perhaps they actually spoke like this, or if the narrator is reporting their speech in his own idiolect, as he would naturally do. This draws our attention to the power of language and the nature of truth.

Until line 44, the customers are referred to as 'di shoppers'. At this point, however, they are changed into 'yoo shoppers'. Suddenly the reader is located within the poem, taking on the role of the customers. These are the characters for whom the narrator has shown little respect throughout, neglecting them to be with his bride. Now, the couple feel the freedom and control to come downstairs together only once the shoppers are no longer there to disturb them. Why do you think the poet chooses this moment, when the customers are clearly identified as unwanted outsiders, to identify them with us the readers?

Ideas to consider

In some ways the couple have a limited life. The bride remains in the flat above the shop, venturing as far as the shop itself only once the customers have left and it is closed. Yet she expresses herself freely without being restricted by someone else's ideas of what would be appropriate; and has contact with the world beyond the shop via the internet. The couple's relationship appears to transcend the world

Key quotation

tiny eyes ov a gun

and di tummy ov a teddy

(ll. 28–29)

Build critical skills

Look out for ways that links are created between words through rhyme. For example at the end of lines in the fifth stanza 'daddy' is related to 'Punjabi' by rhyme but to 'drunk' by alliteration. Also think about repetition. Why do you think 'my bride' is repeated at the start of three consecutive stanzas? Why do the last four stanzas begin with the same words?

of the shop. They look 'past' the signs in the window. Whereas the narrator's interaction with the customers is exclusively about money transactions, the conversation between the couple parodies the idea of buying and selling and ends with the idea that some things are priceless. What do you think this tells us about the value of love; and about the inner life of the shopkeeper? What does it disclose about the narrator's second-generation attitude towards the business that his father worked to establish?

'Climbing My Grandfather' by Andrew Waterhouse

Context

The concern with both family relationships and the landscape that we find in 'Climbing My Grandfather' can be seen elsewhere in Andrew Waterhouse's life and writing. He published his first collection of poetry, *In*, for which he won the Forward Prize for Best First Collection, in 2000. He was collecting poems to go into a second anthology before his suicide in 2001 and this was published posthumously in 2002, entitled *2nd*. In these poems, he often deals with his family relationships, for example his father's gardening; you might like to use these to compare the grandfather's 'earth-stained hand' (l. 7).

Andrew Waterhouse was a committed environmentalist throughout his life, and became a lecturer in Environmental Studies. As a teenager, he asked his family to buy him areas of rainforest as birthday gifts and later he took part in the Trees for Life programme that works to restore forest in the Scottish Highlands. In 1998 he bought ten acres of land and began to plant a wood on it. He wrote articles for environmental magazines and walking guides.

> **Glossary**
>
> **brogues (l. 2):** strong outdoor shoes with a pattern made by small holes
>
> **traverse (l. 6):** here, means to travel sideways
>
> **screed (l. 18):** indicates scree, which is a covering of stones on a mountain slope

What happens?

The speaker describes climbing his grandfather using an extended metaphor of mountain climbing. It is possible to see this as a child climbing on an adult, imaginatively relating it to mountain climbing. Much of the sense of wonder is extremely child-like: 'stare into his brown eyes, watch a pupil / slowly open and close' (ll. 19–20). Yet we can also view it as in the voice of an adult, possibly an experienced climber, viewing the experience of getting to know his grandfather by comparing it to climbing. The terminology is often beyond the reach of a young child: 'traverse' (l. 6), 'good purchase' (l. 8), 'altitude' (l. 23). Do you think it might also be possible to view it as the speaker literally climbing a mountain but viewing this as a metaphor for the growing relationship with his grandfather? There are several mountains or natural rock formations with names including 'The Old Man of', such as The Old Man of Coniston in Lancashire or The Old Man of Storr on the Isle of Skye.

Structure

The poem tracks the speaker climbing the grandfather, with the structure of the poem following the stages in the climb. As the reader progresses through the poem, the speaker's climb up the grandfather likewise progresses. The use of one single stanza gives a sense of unity and harmony to the poem: the grandfather is there for the speaker without interruption. Enjambment is often used to give a sense of steady progress and to reflect the climbing motion. Look, for example, at lines 15–16: 'then pull / myself up the loose skin'. Just as the speaker pulls himself up a level, the poem progresses a level into the next line. Try to find your own examples; you might want to investigate lines 20–21.

This enjambment is combined with caesurae to break up the formal shape of the poem so that it has a more casual, conversational feel. Sometimes, as in line 20, the caesura of a full stop also slows the pace. Look at the way that this is combined with long vowel assonance in this line to achieve this effect: 'slowly open and close. Then up over'. This can convey the grandson pausing with the effort of climbing, the tolerant acceptance of the grandfather, and the depth of the bond between them.

At the same time, there are important points where an end-stopped line is used. The opening is exactly one sentence long: 'I decide to do it free, without a rope or net.' This sentence establishes a mystery by not immediately clarifying what 'it' is. There is no specific mention of the grandfather in this first line. So at this point it is all about the speaker on his own, deciding how to approach the climb, more than about the relationship with the grandfather. This is emphasised by the first word being 'I', which is then echoed in the assonance of the *i* in the second syllable of 'dec*i*de'. This is very different from the ending of the poem, where the speaker has bonded so completely with the grandfather that he is able to use the certainty word 'knowing' to describe his understanding of him. In this way the structure of the poem shows how their relationship has developed.

Language and imagery

You might like to think about why a small child would consider a mountain as an appropriate metaphor for the grandfather. What is it about the size and age of the grandfather compared to the child that encourages the grandchild to see him in this way?

You could also think about why the poem uses the present tense throughout. It gives a sense of immediacy, which helps express the closeness between the child and the grandfather. Does it also create ambiguity about when this 'climb' takes place? It could be a single event of a young child literally climbing on his grandfather's body, or it could be a metaphor for the grandson coming to know the grandfather throughout all the years of their relationship.

The poem often generates imagery through patterns in the sounds of words. Consider the short vowel assonance in line 9: 'the sk*i*n of h*i*s f*i*nger *i*s smooth and th*i*ck'. This helps to keep the line light, so as to avoid any suggestion of unpleasant toughness about the thick skin. It also offers a mood of unity and harmony.

Key quotation

the skin of his finger is smooth and thick

like warm ice.
(ll. 9–10)

You could explore the patterns of sounds in 'I cross the screed cheek' (l. 18), such as the long vowel assonance in 'screed cheek'. Scree can be hazardous; as a metaphor for stubble or a beard, then, it also suggests that the cheek is rough and needs to be approached with care. This reflects the cautious, attentive climbing, but also the loving attention shown to the grandfather. You could also consider the consonance of the hard *k* sound: '**c**ross the s**c**reed chee**k**'. You might feel that it is possible to hear the sounds of clinking climbing equipment here.

> **GRADE** *BOOSTER*
>
> When choosing quotations to learn, try to concentrate on those about which you can say several things. This will make the revision process easier. It will also help you to analyse in depth in the exam: it is better to make fewer points and explore each in detail than to make a huge number of points but consider each only superficially.

Ideas to consider

The grandfather does not move in this poem and is given no words to speak. Yet at the same time it feels extremely intimate – and there is a sense of the speaker having come to know him fully by the end. How do you feel that we are able to get to know the grandfather throughout? Do we have a detailed sense of him as an individual? Think what we can learn about him from details such as 'the glassy ridge of a scar' (l. 11), the 'earth-stained hand' (l. 7) and the 'splintered' nails (l. 8). How are these suggestive of the speaker's love and respect? Is the poem general enough that we can relate it to our own relationships with loved ones?

REVIEW YOUR LEARNING

(Answers are given on p. 104.)

1 Which of the poets in the *Love and Relationship* cluster are regarded as Romantics?

2 Which two Victorian poets within this cluster were married to each other?

3 Which poem presents the speaker's admiration for his father's skills with a horse plough?

4 Who was appointed Poet Laureate in 2009?

5 a In which country would you find a hill called Skirrid Hill or Skirrid Fawr?

   b Which poem is taken from an anthology called *Skirrid Hill*?

6 In which poem can you find imagery linking a tape measure to both an umbilical cord and to an umbilical cable used by astronauts?

Target your thinking

- What do you understand by the terms 'love' and 'relationship'?
- What aspects of love and relationships might you need to consider in the examination?
- How might you link some of these ideas when comparing the poems?

A key quality that makes an essay stand out to the examiner is the depth of its analysis. The clarity of your thinking, the complexity of your investigation into the issues, and the level of detail at which you are able to compare the texts will all contribute to how far you move up the mark scheme. It will help you prepare for writing your exam response to think carefully about why these poems have been grouped into a single cluster: they all relate in different ways to ideas about love and relationships. Just as in the exam it is essential to analyse the language of the question, investigating love and relationships revolves around exploring the different ways in which these words can be used.

It would be helpful to consider some of the many aspects of love and relationships that might be the focus of your examination question. Below are some suggestions of separate, but related, concepts of love and relationships. You should not feel restricted to these, but instead use them as a springboard to generate more ideas about what these themes mean to you.

Love within romantic relationships

Wanting to be together

When we think about love, one of the first ideas that comes to mind may be that of falling in love. You might like to compare poems that show couples happy in a romantic relationship and individuals for whom the physical presence of the partner is important. You could, for example, link Sonnet 29 'I think of thee!' with 'Singh Song!' How does the shopkeeper's willingness to neglect his work in order to be with his new bride relate to the longing of Sonnet 29's speaker for the actual presence of the lover?

Unfulfilled desire

Other poems look at frustrated love. In 'When We Two Parted', we are offered the viewpoint of the rejected lover; in 'Love's Philosophy' we are offered that of the lover who is attempting to persuade the addressee into a relationship. Think about how both compare to 'Neutral Tones', in which the couple appear simply to have fallen out of love. You might notice that both Byron and Shelley emphasise the intensity of the speaker's emotions, while Hardy is at pains to stress the couple's apathy. It would be interesting to think about how all three poems use pathetic fallacy to convey these feelings. You could also look at how they relate to 'Winter Swans': the natural background is important both as imagery and in inspiring the couple; rather than the grandeur of Shelley's sublime imagery, though, Owen Sheers gives a dignity to the common experience of making up after an argument.

> **Build critical skills**
>
> In only two of the above poems are the words of the romantic partner included: in 'Winter Swans' with 'They mate for life' (l. 13) and in 'Singh Song!' with the concluding dialogue between the shopkeeper and the bride. Does this make a difference to how we see either the partner or the speaker? Is there a difference between the use of speech marks in 'Winter Swans' and the use of italics in 'Singh Song!'?

'Porphyria's Lover' and 'The Farmer's Bride' bring in a further dimension: when desire for the lover is prompted by, or pushed to the point at which it leads to, mental illness.

Love within family relationships

Many of the poems deal with relationships between parents and children: think about 'Follower', 'Before You Were Mine', 'Walking Away', 'Eden

> **Build critical skills**
>
> Do you think that the relationship in these poems is equal? Does the bride in 'Singh Song!' seem as desperate to be with her husband as he is to be with her? In Sonnet 29 does the lover, presented as the mighty tree, seem to need the speaker as she does him? If there is an imbalance, do you think this suggests that one partner loves the other more? Or is it to do with the fact that we only hear one partner speak about their feelings for the other?

Rock' and 'Mother, Any Distance'. In addition, 'Climbing My Grandfather' explores love between a grandchild and grandparent. You should notice that only 'Walking Away' is written from the point of view of the parent; for the remainder the persona is the child (or grandchild). Central to all of these poems is the way that these relationships change over time, particularly as a result of the ageing process. In 'Walking Away' and 'Mother, Any Distance', the change is brought about as a result of the child's increasing independence. Both imply that one way in which parents show love is through allowing the child the freedom to move away from them. Time is again crucial in 'Before You Were Mine', but here because of the child's feelings about being unable to know the mother before her own birth. Instead of the child wanting more freedom, she is seeking a more intimate relationship with the mother. It is the mother who is presented in the poem as the young woman who is free because she is not tied down by a relationship. The poem gives this an additional twist by pointing out that the mother is also a daughter, and at that time was seeking independence from her own mother, the speaker's grandmother: 'your Ma stands at the close / with a hiding for the late one.' (ll. 9–10).

You might like to compare poems in which the child becomes more independent, such as 'Climbing My Grandfather', in which the child becomes more intimately acquainted with the grandfather as the poem progresses. You could also explore ways in which love is presented as the same as or different from dependence. Is it possible for a child to need the parent less and yet love the parent more or simply in a different way? Is the parent in 'Mother, Any Distance' helping the child to become independent or is she clinging on? How does the speaker feel about this? What does the role reversal in the final stanza of 'Follower' have to say? Does the fact that the father now 'will not go away' (l. 24) indicate that the speaker feels pestered by him or that he has the reassurance that his father will always be there, or both?

You could also think about how poems that idealise the parents, such as 'Eden Rock', 'Follower' and 'Before You Were Mine', compare with those where the younger generation rebels. In 'Singh Song!' we see the bride's disrespect for her parents-in-law. What does it tell us that the speaker passes no comment on this? Does it indicate that he endorses the rebellion? To what extent is the speaker economically dependent upon his father, in running one of his shops and living above it? What attitude does he reveal towards his parents through his approach towards managing the shop? In 'Walking Away', do you think the child is actively rebelling against the parent, or does it just feel this way from the parent's perspective?

Build critical skills

How does 'Eden Rock' relate to these ideas? On one level it is a nostalgic reminiscence stimulated by childhood memory. It is a recollection of perfect happiness within the presence of the parents; yet this is in the irretrievable past and so expresses something that is not available to the speaker now. If we regard it as a metaphor for the parents calling the speaker into life before his birth, or calling him towards death, then it expresses instead a longing for an intimate relationship that the speaker hopes to achieve in the future.

The relationship between humans and nature

'Letters from Yorkshire' presents a man who shows a genuine love of nature. He works outside with his hands and is inspired to write to the speaker by witnessing the arrival of the lapwings. You might compare this with 'Follower', where the speaker reveres the father's understanding of the land and his horses. Think also about the grandfather's 'earth-stained hand' (l. 7) in 'Climbing My Grandfather', and why the metaphor of mountain climbing appeals to the speaker. You could link this to the way that the natural background in 'Winter Swans' not only reflects the couple's mood through the storm, but also inspires them through the swans. How do you think these poems, in which characters literally interact with nature, compare with poems such as 'Love's Philosophy' where the natural imagery is used to persuade or 'Neutral Tones' where it reflects the characters' moods?

Relationships through writing

An important feature of the relationship in 'Letters from Yorkshire' is that it is conducted at a distance, through the medium of writing. You might want to bring in the context of Elizabeth Barrett Browning's relationship with Robert Browning, which began with a letter and was continued partly through the writing of her sonnets, including Sonnet 29. How does this compare to poems that are expressed to a specific reader: the 'thou' of 'When We Two Parted' or 'Love's Philosophy', or the 'you' of 'Neutral Tones', 'Walking Away', 'Before You Were Mine', 'Winter Swans' or 'Mother, Any Distance'?

The relationship between different religious ideas

You could investigate poems that place the relationships within a religious context. 'Eden Rock' draws upon Christian imagery, hinting at the possibility of achieving heaven through the speaker's relationship with his parents. 'Walking Away' draws parallels between the father's need to release the son and God, suggesting the relationship within Christianity between God the Father and God the Son. You might compare this with the way that the idea of 'a law divine' (l. 6) is used persuasively in 'Love's Philosophy'. What about the 'God-curst sun' (l. 15) of 'Neutral Tones'?

Build critical skills

Think about the interaction between the characters and nature in 'The Farmer's Bride'. The farmer measures everything in terms of seasons and the landscape, as is consistent with his profession. The bride is throughout related to natural imagery; do you think this reflects how she really is or how the farmer sees her? Does the poem leave it deliberately unclear?

Build critical skills

Think about the last line of 'Porphyria's Lover': 'And yet God has not said a word!' Is the speaker challenging God? Does he think that he somehow has been victorious? Is he so disturbed as to think he has done nothing sinful?

REVIEW YOUR LEARNING

(Answers are given on p. 104.)

1 Which poems show a speaker driven by the desire to be with their romantic partner?

2 Which poems look at mental illness within the context of romantic relationships?

3 Which poem is written from the point of view of a parent watching their child become more independent?

4 In which poem will you find climbing used as a metaphor for an increasingly intimate relationship?

5 How do you think you might describe the bride's attitude towards her parents-in-law in 'Singh Song!'?

Assessment Objectives and skills

Target your thinking

- What do the different Assessment Objectives refer to?
- Which Assessment Objectives are used to assess Section B?
- Which Assessment Objectives are important for Section C?

Which Assessment Objectives apply to the poetry questions?

As you are aware, the poetry questions are in Section B and Section C of Paper 2 of your examination. There are four Assessment Objectives (or AOs for short) altogether for the English literature GCSE. You will be assessed on three of these for Section B (comparing the poems you have studied in class) and two of them for Section C (the Unseen poems).

For **Section B** the relevant Assessment Objectives are worded as follows:

AO1 Read, understand and respond to texts. Students should be able to:
- maintain a critical style and develop an informed personal response
- use textual references, including quotations, to support and illustrate interpretations.

AO2 Analyse the language, form and structure used by a writer to create meanings and effects, using relevant subject terminology where appropriate.

AO3 Show understanding of the relationship between texts and the contexts in which they were written.

For **Section C** you will be assessed on AO1 and AO2 only.

You can see that broadly AO1 is about forming and expressing your own interpretation of the poems and using evidence from the poems to back this up.

AO2 is where you will pick up marks by looking at writers' methods. Notice that it refers to 'using relevant subject terminology *where appropriate*'. This means that you shouldn't throw in terms like alliteration or caesura just for their own sake, but because they help you express a relevant point. If you use subject terminology only to label a method, without identifying the effect and relating it to the meaning, this will be worth very few marks. For example, if you said that 'Porphyria's Lover' is in iambic tetrameter, you would not do as well as someone who builds this into a discussion about the effects of this and how it relates to your interpretation of the poem's ideas. Bear in mind that while this AO is about analysing the language, form and structure of poems, it also asks you to link these to the meanings and effects.

For Section B and for the second question on Section C you need to compare poems; AO2 is the only Assessment Objective that your ability to compare will be assessed against in Section C.

AO3 asks you to relate the poems to their contexts. This is kept very broad because what is relevant will depend on the poem, the issues it deals with and the time in which it was written.

AO4 is not covered on the poetry section. You might be aware that there is a further Assessment Objective, AO4, which is used to assess your vocabulary, sentence structures, spelling and punctuation. AO4 is not assessed on Sections B and C of this paper. It is applied only to Section A, when you are answering on your prose text. This, of course, doesn't mean that you shouldn't think about your writing style when you are answering on the poetry questions. Often the more sophisticated your writing style, the more perceptive your response can appear. Moreover, it will help you with part of AO1 (maintaining a critical style and developing an informed personal response) if you demonstrate strong writing skills in structuring your essay and arguing for your interpretation of the poems.

An important point is that you won't be marked down for spelling on the poetry sections. In Section A, if you have thought of an excellent word to express your ideas but aren't sure how to spell it, you might need to weigh up the advantage of using the word versus the risk of weakening the examiner's perception of your spelling skills. In Sections B and C, however, the absence of AO4 means it would be better to use the word because you won't lose marks for a spelling error.

Weighting of the AOs

Section B is worth a total of 30 marks, and this is weighted with 12 marks for AO1, 12 marks for AO2 and 6 marks for AO3. This means that you should cover all three Assessment Objectives, but remember that AO1 and AO2 are each worth twice as many marks as AO3.

Section C is divided into two questions. The first, where you analyse one Unseen poem, is worth 24 marks. Half of these are for AO1 and half are for AO2. The second question, where you compare two Unseen poems, is assessed on AO2 only and is worth 8 marks.

REVIEW YOUR LEARNING

(Answers are given on p. 104.)

1 What is AO1 assessing?
2 What sort of material do you need to consider to successfully address AO2?
3 What do you understand by the term 'AO3'?
4 Which AOs are assessed in Section B: the Anthology poems?
5 Which AOs do you need to consider in the first part of Section C?
6 Which is the only AO that is assessed when comparing the two Unseen poems?

Tackling the exams

Target your thinking

- What sorts of questions will you have to answer in Section B and Section C?
- What is the best way to plan your answers?
- What is the best way to revise for Section B?
- How do you deal with the Unseen poems?

Section B – the Anthology

What you will be asked to do

For Section B you will be asked to compare two poems. One of the poems will be named, and this will be printed in the exam paper. You will be able to choose a poem from the same cluster to compare with this. Other than the named poem, the fourteen poems from your cluster will *not* be printed in the exam. This means that you will need to know them all extremely thoroughly in order to be able to make accurate textual references, including quotations. This means not just remembering the words in the quote, but making sure the punctuation and line breaks are exactly right, because without these you won't be able to discuss the structure of the poem so effectively. The titles of the fourteen poems will be listed on the examination paper, to help you recall them and decide which will be most suitable to compare with the named poem for this question.

See the previous chapter for the three Assessment Objectives that apply to this section of the exam paper.

How to tackle the question

Answer the question set

Some candidates find it tempting to write down everything they can remember about each of the poems. After all, you have worked so hard to revise so many different points that you may feel desperate to demonstrate all of this knowledge, even if it isn't relevant to the question. There are, though, two key reasons why this will in fact tend to lower your mark.

First, the examiner can only award marks for material that answers the question. Writing about anything else just uses up precious time in the exam. Rather than dazzling the examiner with the breadth of your knowledge, you are instead likely to give the impression you know so little that you didn't have enough ideas for the actual question and so had to pad it out with irrelevant points.

Second, the wording of the question will be designed to draw your attention to the three Assessment Objectives. Take, for example, the following question:

> Compare the ways writers present ideas about the treatment of women in 'Porphyria's Lover' and in one other poem from 'Love and Relationships'.

The first word of the question tells you to *compare*. This is part of AO1. By asking you about how poets *present* their ideas you are being drawn to AO2, meaning you deal with writers' methods. The word *ideas* is designed to make you think about the context (AO3). As such, if you read the question and think carefully about what it is asking you to do, then this will lead you to target the criteria of the mark scheme.

Develop a line of argument

The top end of the mark scheme is looking for a well-structured argument. Some candidates will make a number of separate points that are all excellent in themselves but don't work together to answer the question. You can take this to the next level if you link them together, so that each paragraph builds on the preceding one. Use your topic sentence at the start of each paragraph to show how what you are about to say links to the points you have already made, and how it answers the question. Then finish each paragraph with a short sentence pulling together your points so far, again referring this back to the question.

There are several different ways to structure your essay, each of which has advantages and disadvantages. You need to be aware that although the mark scheme is divided into AOs, this doesn't require you to separate your essay into three different sections, one on each Assessment Objective. Some candidates do use this approach: they deal with ideas, then techniques, then context. This strategy is likely to favour weaker candidates who are concerned that without it they may forget to include one of the AOs. While it is possible for a highly skilled candidate to do well in this way, you are likely to run the risk of your essay looking somewhat mechanical. Your answer will appear more sophisticated if you blend the ideas in the poem with the ways in which the poet's methods achieve their effects, and enrich this by placing your analysis within the contexts of the poems. This is particularly relevant for AO2 because of the way that this specifically links language, form and structure to the way writers use these to create meanings and effects. An approach that blends a discussion of meanings with the way that writers employ different techniques to evoke these should be best positioned to cover all the elements of this AO. This strategy is demonstrated in the sample answers you will find on page 72.

Keep it comparative

Many candidates underperform because, although they offer an excellent analysis of each of the poems individually, they effectively write two separate essays, one on each poem. The essential element of the task, triggered by the first word of the question, is to *compare*. An effective strategy is to make sure you deal with both poems in each paragraph, consistently drawing comparisons. Use each topic sentence to outline how the points you will be making about each poem individually relate to each other. This will help to keep you focused on comparison throughout. By using the final sentence of the paragraph to keep answering the question, you additionally will ensure that it remains comparative.

It is crucial to remember that comparison means discussing not only how the poems are the same, but also how they are different. As part of this, you may be able to say that a particular aspect of the poems is similar in one way but quite opposed in another. For example, you might find that the poems express similar ideas but use very different techniques; or that a similar technique is used to very different effect in the two poems.

Subject terminology

At the top end of the mark scheme, AO2 requires a *judicious* use of subject terminology. This means it is essential to integrate the language of poetic techniques into the points you are making about the effects of the poem and the writers' ideas. You should avoid 'technique spotting', where candidates simply name a technique used but don't go on to discuss it in their analysis.

Context

What counts as context is kept deliberately broad, because it can cover such a huge range, depending on the poem and the question. Even here, your approach should ideally be comparative. So you can look for ways in which the contexts make the poems both similar and different.

The different time periods in which texts are written or the different cultural backgrounds of their poets might be relevant for you. For example, Byron and Shelley are both writing within the Romantic tradition. Other poets, such as Daljit Nagra, write about clashes of culture within modern Britain.

One relevant way to consider context is to discuss the extent to which a poem transcends its particular historical and cultural circumstances. For example, Sonnet 29 can be viewed as part of the Barrett Browning love story, but it also expresses universal values about the nature of love.

Plan

The key to getting all of this right is to plan in the exam. Your plan is written for your benefit rather than for the examiner, so it should be something that works for *you*. It doesn't need to take that long to write. Some people prefer diagrammatic plans, such as spider diagrams; others prefer to order points in a short list. The key thing is that this is where you decide which of the points you have revised are relevant to the question and also the order you will put them in to present a coherent line of argument.

Revise in a comparative way

Although you can, of course, plan your answer to the question set only once you are in the exam room, you can pave the way for this by the way you revise. Candidates who revise each poem individually, without thinking about how to compare them, will have to do all the work of deciding points of similarity and difference in the exam room. Instead, you can revise poems both individually and by drawing up charts that highlight points of comparison. This way, when you plan in the exam, you just need to decide which of your comparison points are relevant to the question set and then link them together into a coherent argument.

Remember, though, that each poem can be compared interestingly with more than one other from the cluster. Deciding which is the most suitable will depend on the question set, so you will need to compose several revision charts that link each poem with a number of others.

The table below shows how part of a revision chart might look like for a comparison of 'Porphyria's Lover' with 'The Farmer's Bride'.

'Porphyria's Lover'	'The Farmer's Bride'
Written and published in Victorian period. Published under three different titles.	Published in 1912 but written during Victorian period.
Woman criticised for being powerful and forward. Does not satisfy stereotype for ideal unmarried woman.	Bride criticised for not meeting her husband's expectations and needs. Does not satisfy stereotype for ideal married woman.
Male speaker controls language. Porphyria's words are presented in indirect speech. He chooses the words and so controls how she is seen.	Bride is given no speech in the poem. There is what at first appears to be direct speech, but this is the farmer describing her facial expression.

GRADE *FOCUS*:

Grade 5

In order to achieve a Grade 5 in Section B a candidate must be able to:

- develop a clear personal response to their chosen poems
- show a clear understanding of the ways in which the poets use language, form and structure to create effects for the reader
- use appropriate textual references to support their ideas
- show a clear understanding of the importance of contexts
- make clear and credible comparisons between their chosen poems.

Grade 8

In order to achieve a Grade 8 in Section B a candidate must be able to:

- sustain a convincing personal response to their chosen poems
- produce a perceptive analysis of the ways in which the poets use language, form and structure to create effects for the reader
- use judicious and well-integrated textual references
- show a perceptive awareness of the importance of contexts in shaping meanings and responses
- make perceptive and convincing comparisons between their chosen poems.

REVIEW YOUR LEARNING (SECTION B)

(Answers are given on p. 104.)

1 How many poems will you have to compare in Section B?
2 Will the named poem be printed on the exam paper?
3 What will the first word of the question ask you to do?
4 What would be the most effective revision technique for Section B?
5 What is 'technique spotting'?

Section C – the Unseen

What you will be asked to do

There will be two questions in Section C, which deals with Unseen poetry.

The first will ask you a specific question about one poem and is worth 24 marks. You will be marked on Assessment Objectives 1 and 2.

The second will ask you to compare the first poem with another poem on a similar theme, but here you will be marked only on Assessment Objective 2. Be careful, though: this doesn't mean just identifying writers' techniques, it also means thinking about the *effect* they have on you.

How to feel confident about a poem you are not familiar with

Many candidates panic at the thought of the Unseen, which leads them to underperform and waste time. Yet there is every reason for you to be confident.

First, this is a skills-based exam. You simply will not have time to write about every single detail of the poem in full. Nobody could – and nobody is expecting you to. Instead, you need to show the *skills* for a particular grade. It is quite likely that there will be aspects of the poem you are unsure of within the constraints of the exam; you can still demonstrate the necessary skills on the parts you are more confident about.

Second, a poem is brought to life by the act of reading it. Each of us adds our own personality and experiences to a poem, so for each of us its meaning will be slightly different. The examiner is interested in what the poem means to *you*. Your objective is to answer the question set with your interpretation of the poem, and to justify this with close analysis of the language, structure and form, supported by textual references. Remember that Assessment Objective 1 asks for an informed *personal* response.

Some candidates find it both frustrating and concerning that there is no single right answer. Yet you should find that this offers you freedom. Obviously, it is possible to be wrong about a poem if you make a claim that is simply untrue: to take an example you will be familiar with from the Anthology, if a candidate claimed that 'Love's Philosophy' was about ballet dancing while eating ice cream, this would simply be wrong. Candidates can, however, disagree about the effect that a particular poetic technique has for them and still be able to justify their responses skilfully. Let's look at the last two lines of 'Love's Philosophy':

> What is all this sweet work worth
>
> If thou kiss not me?
>
> (ll. 15–16)

Different candidates may notice that the whole of this is in monosyllables. They may also be interested in the repetition of *w* in '**W**hat is all this s**w**eet **w**ork **w**orth' and the similarities in the sounds of the words 'work' and 'worth'.

Suppose Candidate A decides that this makes the speaker's love seem pure and honest. (S)he may argue that the simple language suggests the feelings are genuine and that the soft, echoing *w* sound gives a sense of gentle and sincere love. Candidate B might say instead that it feels resentful and desperate. (S)he might suggest that the monosyllables make the tone feel harsh and that the repetition in the sounds feels like the speaker is running out of arguments and so becoming repetitive.

Even though the two candidates have formed apparently opposed personal responses to the poem, it is not the case that one is right and the other is wrong. It is what the candidates do with their ideas that determines how far they climb up the mark scheme. The key for both candidates would be to blend their ideas about language, structure and form with their description of the effects, so that all the time they are justifying how the poem makes them feel by detailed analysis. To maximise the marks they can gain from their ideas, they should make their analysis part of a well-structured argument so that their individual ideas build on each other.

Of course, Candidate C may offer a yet-more-sophisticated response by arguing that both interpretations are simultaneously true. (S)he might develop an idea that the speaker feels a sincere and deep love, but is frustrated by the fear that this may not be returned. This would be more evidence to the examiner of exploratory thought because it considers alternative readings.

By contrast, a candidate who simply identifies that there are some monosyllables and some consonance, without going on to talk about the effects, would be working at the lower end of the mark scheme. Remember that although you are asked to use appropriate subject terminology, this is in order to provide a scaffolding for your response about how the author is using these techniques to shape meanings and effects.

So, decide how the poem makes you feel; pick out features of the language, structure and form that support your interpretation; and explain clearly how these work together to make you feel that way.

Strategy for Section C – the Unseen

Answer the question

The Unseen can easily tempt candidates to write down everything they think of; it is crucial, however, to focus in on the question. Just think how frustrating it would be if you asked someone whether they wanted to go to the cinema, and they gave you a complete history of film-making but failed to answer yes or no! This means that as you read the poems, you should have the exam questions in mind.

Remember you have two questions: the first on one of the poems and the second comparing both poems. Start by reading the first question and then annotating the relevant poem with points for that question. Because this question covers AOs 1 and 2, you will be looking for points about ideas and meanings as well as the language, structure and form. The question will tell you which aspect of the text it wants you to explore.

When you are ready to start the second question, read both poems, all the time thinking only about points of comparison. It is crucial to remember that this means differences as well as similarities. Because you are not marked on AO1 in this question, confine your comparison to the writers' methods (AO2) but remember that this includes the *effects* of the methods.

Read each poem more than once

Although you are under time pressure in the exam, it is essential to develop your understanding of the poems before you start to write. Do not expect to be able to grasp the poems by reading them once: it will be your re-reading that provides your most sophisticated points.

You are assessed on the quality of your response and not on its length. So a candidate whose points are fewer in number but of higher quality will find it much easier to impress the examiner than one who writes a huge number of points that only just graze the superficial level of the poem.

Plan

Planning is especially important for the Unseen, where you have not had the opportunity to formulate an interpretation before the exam. There are two extreme examples of planning that prevent candidates from achieving as well as they could:

- The first is no plan. Candidates who do this tend to rush straight in, without thinking about how ideas link together, and so have no coherent response. In certain cases candidates even change their minds as they write and end up contradicting themselves. They are also likely to repeat themselves, which wastes more time than would have been spent writing an effective plan.
- The second is a lengthy, detailed plan, which is really a mini-essay. Candidates who do this essentially write the same essay twice, and so cut in half the time they have.

Instead, your plan should be a concise outline of your strategy. Decide which of your ideas go in which section of your essay. You don't need to write this out in full in your plan. You can simply allocate each section of the essay a number, and then write that number next to any annotations on the poems that go with that section. Alternatively, you might like to highlight the annotations you have made on the poems in different colours and just write the name of the colour on your plan. It would just be a waste of time to write quotes in full in the plan.

Some people like to plan in a diagrammatic way, such as a spider diagram. Others prefer a more linear approach, such as a list. It is entirely your choice: try different methods as you revise and find which works for you.

GRADE *FOCUS*:

Grade 5

In order to achieve a Grade 5 in Section C a candidate must be able to:

- develop a clear personal response to the Unseen poem in Question 1
- show a clear understanding of the ways in which the poets use language, form and structure to create effects for the reader in both Unseen poems
- use appropriate textual references to support their ideas
- make clear and credible comparisons of the methods used in the two poems in Question 2.

Grade 8

In order to achieve a Grade 8 in Section C a candidate must be able to:

- sustain a convincing personal response to the Unseen poem in Question 1
- produce a perceptive analysis of the ways in which the poets use language, form and structure to create effects for the reader in both Unseen poems
- use judicious and well-integrated textual references
- make perceptive and convincing comparisons of the methods used in the two poems in Question 2.

REVIEW YOUR LEARNING (SECTION C)

(Answers are given on p.104.)

1 How many questions will you need to answer on Unseen poetry for Section C of your exam?

2 How many poems will you need to write about for Question 1?

3 How many poems will you need to write about for Question 2?

4 Why should you read each poem more than once?

5 What are the dangers of having no plan?

Writing your answer – Sections B and C

Now you are ready to start writing your answer. The first thing to remember is that you are working against the clock and so it's really important to use your time wisely.

It is possible that you may not have time to deal with all of the points you wish to make in your response. The idea is to *select* the ones that you find most interesting and to develop them in a sustained and detailed manner. In order to move up the levels in the mark scheme, it is important to write a lot about a little, rather than a little about a lot.

You must also remember to address the *whole question*, as you will be penalised if you fail to do so.

If you have any time left at the end of the examination, do not waste it! Check carefully that your meaning is clear and that you have done the very best you can. Look back at your plan and check that you have included all your best points. Is there anything else you can add? Keep thinking until you are told to put your pen down!

Key points to remember:

- Do not just jump straight in! Spending time wisely in the first moments may gain you extra marks later.
- Write a brief plan.
- Remember to answer all parts of the question.
- Use your time wisely! Try to leave a few minutes at the end to look back over your work and check your spelling, punctuation and grammar, so that your meaning is clear and so that you know that have done the very best that you can.
- Keep an eye on the clock!

Sample essays for Section B – the Anthology

Now let us look at how two candidates use ideas such as those in the previous chapter to form the basis of their responses to two questions. For the first question they will both be comparing 'Porphyria's Lover' and 'The Farmer's Bride'; for the second they will both be comparing 'Mother, Any Distance' with 'Walking Away'. In each of the responses, Candidate X fulfils all of the criteria for Grade 5 and is beginning to show evidence of Grade 6. Candidate Y, meanwhile, fulfils all of the criteria for Grade 8 and is starting to move into Grade 9.

First question

We will start with the candidates' responses to the following question:

> Compare the ways poets present ideas about the treatment of women in 'Porphyria's Lover' and in one other poem from 'Love and Relationships'.

Although Candidate X is overall working at Grade 5, in this introduction (s)he demonstrates a lower standard:

Robert Browning was born in 1812 and died in 1889. He was educated mostly at home. His early poetry was not very successful, so he tried writing drama. This also was not very popular, so he began writing poetry again. He is famous for writing dramatic monologues and 'Porphyria's Lover' is one of the first ones he published. Charlotte Mew lived from 1869 to 1928. Two of her siblings were committed to mental institutions, so she had a strong interest in insanity, which links her to the way Browning explores mental disorders in his dramatic monologues.

1 Seeks to gain marks for context but doesn't keep the points related to the poems or the question.

2 Moves into talking about the poem, but still does not answer the question.

3 While the strength of this sentence is that it begins to compare, this is not done in a way that is relevant to the question.

Compare this with the opening of Candidate Y:

> 'Porphyria's Lover' and 'The Farmer's Bride', the second published in 1912 but written in the nineteenth century, both explore the suppression of the female voice in Victorian times. Just as so many women writers, such as the Brontë sisters, felt able to publish only under a male name, both of the women in these poems are denied the opportunity to speak for themselves. Porphyria's words are presented in indirect speech: 'Murmuring how she loved me – she / Too weak.' Browning uses enjambment to make 'Murmuring ' stand out because it is at the start of the line. It helps to show that the speaker isn't really interested in what Porphyria has to say. The farmer appears to make an opposite complaint regarding the bride: that she fails to speak, 'I've hardly heard her speak at all.' Because the word 'I've' is in italics, however, we can see the similarity in the treatment of the two women. The farmer is bothered that she doesn't focus her attention on him, so both women are criticised by a man because they do not see him as more important than anything else. The farmer's description of the bride's language in 'Happy enough to chat and play' is patronising as it suggests that her language is trivial.

2 Immediately links the point to the language of the poems with a relevant quotation.

4 Picks up the language of the question to show focus.

1 Opens by establishing the relevant context with a point linked to the question.

3 Maintains comparison when analysing quotes.

Candidate X continues:

1 Now begins to focus in on the question and to relate this to the form of the poems. This would probably make a better opening paragraph!

2 Comparative.

> Both of these poems are dramatic monologues spoken by men. This means that the poems focus not on the women directly but on how the men treat the women. We might expect this to mean that the reader is made to agree with the criticisms of the women, but both poems actually do the opposite. In PL this is partly because of the speaker's murder of Porphyria, but we are also given other clues that his

4 Extends this to structure, but could be improved by developing this point further, for example by looking at where the repeated references to hair come in the poem and how the speaker treats Porphyria.

5 Good use of textual support here. It would gain more marks, though, if the language of the quotes was analysed.

criticisms of Porphyria are unfair. He describes her as if she flirts too much and is a corrupt woman. Browning does this by using words his readers would associate with sexual impurity, like 'fall' for her hair and 'soiled' for her gloves. However the person who is obsessed with the hair isn't Porphyria but the speaker. We can see this because he uses it to strangle her and also because he uses the word 'hair' four times in the poem. The bride in FB also doesn't get to speak for herself. The only time that she is described as speaking is to animals: 'chat and play / With birds and rabbits'. Other people speak about her: '"Out 'mong the sheep, her be," they said', which stresses the fact that she doesn't have any words in the poem. So the two poems show us the unfairness in the treatment of women, because they don't get to speak for themselves.

3 Relates ideas about the language to the form.

6 Effectively summarises the paragraph to show how it is answering the question.

Now let us see how Candidate Y develops similar ideas. There is more detailed analysis of the quotations as well as a brief, relevant reference to context:

2 Focuses on points of comparison and contrast.

Both poets use dramatic monologues to demonstrate this suppression of women, since both speakers are unreliable narrators. Because neither woman is presented to the reader directly, but only through the speaker, we can never be certain if any statements about them are accurate or just how the speakers see them. Unlike Porphyria, the bride appears at first to be permitted direct speech: 'Not near, not near!' In fact, however, these are not the bride's actual words, but the farmer's interpretation of her facial expression. It continues 'her eyes beseech'. He therefore is not giving but taking power from her. The language used to describe Porphyria indicates that she is flirtatious: 'And made her smooth white shoulder bare'. A Victorian woman would be expected to bare her flesh in

1 Links paragraphs together so that there is a single line of argument for the whole essay.

3 This could be improved by making a clearer link to show how this relates to the point just made about 'The Farmer's Bride'.

4 This weaves in a point about context, but it is very vague. It would be improved if the candidate had been able to refer to some specific evidence for this point.

this way only before her husband. He sees her hair as a symbol of overt sexuality, since 'she let [it] fall'. 'Fall' was a word used by Victorians to indicate a woman who was sexually impure. Porphyria's actions, however, don't really look like an attempt to be seductive. The first thing she does is 'shut the cold out' to bring comfort. In many ways this suggests the Victorian ideal woman, 'The Angel in the House' (as shown in Coventry Patmore's poem of that name) who puts a man's physical and emotional comfort before her own and meets his needs by the way she runs the house. She attends to 'the cheerless grate', making 'all the cottage warm'. The reader is therefore unable to decide what Porphyria is really like. She could actually be how she is described, but she could also be a product of the narrator's imagination, formed from the two stereotypes of the domestic 'Angel' and the promiscuous 'fallen' woman. This is similar to the way that the farmer compares the bride to wild animals or mythical creatures, through similes such as 'a hare', 'a mouse', 'a leveret' and 'a little frightened fay'. She might really be like this, in which case they demonstrate her desire for freedom, but they might merely reflect his attitude towards her. None of the animals he compares her to is domesticated, which could indicate either her failure to become the 'Angel in the House' or that he wishes to domesticate, tame and control her. So in both cases, the reader experiences the negative treatment of women because they are seen only through the eyes of men and are not allowed control over how they are shown in the poem.

5 This reference to context is supported by a specific phrase well-used in Victorian times, deriving from a popular Victorian poem.

6 Builds the comparison by investigating points of similarity, but shows less detail on 'The Farmer's Bride' than on 'Porphyria's Lover'.

Candidate X continues:

> There is a battle between the sexes in both poems. At first Porphyria appears strong; Porphyria moves his limp body: 'She put my arm about her waist'. Because of this, the speaker gains power over her by murdering her. He kills her because he cannot cope with a woman who can make her own decisions. Once he has killed her, he is able to position her body how he likes it, moving her about like a doll: 'I propped her head up as before'. In the same way, in FB the farmer can't stand that the bride doesn't do exactly what he wants and expects from her:
>
> > 'Sweet as the first wild violets, she,
> >
> > To her wild self. But what to me?'
>
> He wants her life to be focused on him, so he can't stand that she is 'Sweet' for herself and not for him. Mew writes the whole line in words of one syllable. This makes it seem more angry and frustrated. The full stop is exactly in the middle of the line, so that the bride is in one half and the farmer is in the other. This shows how separate they are. It shows the farmer's ideas about how women should be treated because he thinks the bride should live for him instead of having what she wants for herself.

1 The paragraph opening clearly identifies the points being made. It could be improved by changing the wording to relate more to the treatment of women than to the relationships between men and women.

2 Well-selected quotations used in support. This could be taken to the next level by analysing them in detail.

3 This is a more effective use of quotation, because several points about the structure are linked, blended together with the ideas.

4 Brings the points back to the question.

Candidate Y continues:

> This relates to the fact that the men treat the women as they do because of a power struggle. The second half of PL mirrors the first, with the speaker mimicking Porphyria's positioning of his body. He now takes control of her as she previously had controlled him: 'I propped her head up'. At the centre of the poem, the speaker realises that Porphyria is strong because she has choice and yet that he has power over her because she loves him.

1 Opens the paragraph with a point similar to Candidate X's response, but the language ties it more closely to the question.

2 Blends together points about ideas and structure, but the structural points remain vague.

He chooses to assert his power while destroying hers by killing her. The farmer likewise seeks to restrain the bride's independence. Just as the lover echoed Porphyria's gestures to gain power over her, the farmer does this with language. The word 'turned' is used first to describe the bride's feelings in 'turned afraid'. It is repeated to describe her being locked away: 'turned the key upon her, fast.' so that now it symbolises her imprisonment. The caesura before 'fast' also helps to emphasise the power he has over her by making this word stand out.

3 Takes the general point of comparison made and examines it, relating the effect of the structure in one poem to the language in the other.

Candidate X now develops the argument:

Both poems show a society that believes women should have less power than men and should be owned by men. The farmer is called the 'Farmer' because people identify who he is and how important he is by his job. The woman is called 'The Farmer's Bride' because the farmer thinks he owns her. He says 'I chose a maid' instead of 'We chose each other.' The farmer is part of the community. He says 'We chased her' and 'We caught her.' This treats the bride like an outsider because she doesn't behave the way the society expects her to. In PL, the woman is the opposite. She is has been at a 'gay feast' while the speaker is lying on his own in the cottage. To be with the speaker, she has to choose to be an outcast from society. She decides she will 'vainer ties dissever'. The bride is treated like a social outcast because she won't be with her husband even though she is expected to because she is married to him. Porphyria is a social outcast because she wants to be with a man she is not married to.

1 Supports point with language.

2 This point is expressed less well, because the point is implicit rather than explained.

3 Effective use of a short, embedded quotation.

4 Now uses language that makes it clearer how the points relate to the question.

5 Expression becomes a little clumsy and long-winded in the last two sentences.

Candidate Y takes similar points but achieves a higher level by expressing them in a more sophisticated way and with more detailed attention to language:

1 Shows how two consecutive paragraphs link together and relate to the question.

The bride's loss of power arises partly from the way she is treated within a male-dominated society. The farmer is identified by his occupation because he is 'the Farmer'; she by her marital status because she is the 'Bride'. The simple, monosyllabic language of 'I chose a maid' emphasises that he does not question whether she also should have the right to choose her husband, or even whether to marry at all. The farmer's power also comes from his participation within a community. He doesn't talk about himself and the bride as 'we' (except when he complains that 'we' are not enough without children). When he does use this word in 'We chased her' and 'We caught her', it refers to him and his community. This is emphasised because the enjambment twice places the word 'We' at the start of the line. He speaks in a regional dialect, as in 'she runned away', which is shared by his community: 'her be'. This contrasts with her isolation. In the final stanza the word 'Alone,' is emphasised because the enjambment places it at the start of the line, and then the caesura separates it from the remainder. She is treated as an outcast because she doesn't conform to the stereotype of a married woman. Porphyria, by contrast, is the one with social connections, rather than the isolated speaker. It is therefore significant that the moment he chooses to kill her is when she tells him she has given this up for him. It helps to make her seem weaker in his eyes. Also one effect of the speaker emphasising that Porphyria is a fallen woman is to make it look like society would reject her.

2 Explains and relates to language.

3 Blends points about structure with those about language.

4 Pulls the points made back to the question.

5 Less detailed on 'Porphyria's Lover'. A more balanced paragraph would enable a better display of Candidate Y's comparative skills.

Candidate X concludes:

> So, in both poems women are treated as less good than men. Both poems are dramatic monologues, so in both we see things through the man's point of view and not the woman's. This shows in both poems that the woman isn't treated fairly. There is a battle between the sexes. In both poems the man wants total power over the woman.

This conclusion repeats points already made to draw the answer together. Candidate Y instead continues to develop the line of argument:

> This relates to the poems' exploration of the hypocrisy in Victorian attitudes towards women: expected to be chaste while unmarried and yet sexually available to their husbands. Porphyria is criticised by the speaker for being an unmarried woman who makes her own choices and seeks out her male partner. Once the speaker is able to control Porphyria's corpse and so to remodel her as he chooses, the imagery of sexual impurity is replaced by 'the blue eyes without a stain'. Porphyria is transformed from the determined character of the first half to the timid female. The farmer's frustration is that even after three years of marriage his wife remains a 'maid' and so has failed to provide him with children. Both men become fixated on the woman's hair as a sign of her sexuality. In the closing of 'her hair, her hair!' the alliteration shows the farmer panting as he finds it harder to show self-control. Porphyria's hair, symbolic of her freedom, is used to force her into submission. Both poems reflect the speaker's view that a woman should be nothing other than a wife and mother, submissive to her husband. Both make the reader reject this view because the speaker's repression of women is so disturbing.

1 Relates ideas back to context.

2 Ties back to a point previously made, but adds a new layer so that there is a line of argument.

3 Compares.

4 Final sentence pulls essay together.

Overall, Candidate X has succeeded in writing a clear response that sustains the comparison and certainly should attain a Grade 5. One way (s)he could improve this would be by making the contextual points more relevant to the question. Candidate Y has produced an essay well deserving of a Grade 8, demonstrating a convincing, personal, comparative response, which uses well-selected quotations as the basis of a perceptive analysis. (S)he might take this up a level by investigating alternative readings more.

Second question

Next we see how the two candidates approach the following question:

> Compare the ways writers present ideas about relationships between parents and children in 'Mother, Any Distance' and in one other poem from 'Love and Relationships'.

Candidate X, again working around Grade 5, offers a more effective introduction than in the essay above:

In this essay I am going to be comparing 'Mother, Any Distance' ('Mother') with 'Walking Away' ('Walking'). Both poems are about a point in time when the child is becoming more independent of the parent, but 'Walking' is written from the parent's point of view and in 'Mother' the speaker is the child. They also both address the other person in the poem as 'you', so that both feel very personal. A difference, though, is that 'Walking' is written as a memory of an event that happened eighteen years earlier but 'Mother' is written as if it is happening now. In 'Walking' the speaker uses the past tense: 'I watched you play'. Then he moves into the present tense with 'I can see' as if the memory is so vivid that it is like it is happening now. The whole of 'Mother' is written in the present tense. It means that the reader is left in suspense at the end. Cecil Day Lewis wrote 'Walking' about his son Sean. He may have been particularly sad about losing the time when his son needed him, because he left his first family and had other children with his second wife.

1 Clearly identifies why the poem chosen is relevant and begins to answer the question straight away.

2 Some appreciation of language.

3 Picks up on differences as well as similarities.

4 Well-selected, short quotations used in support.

5 Comments on the effect of the form, but starts to move away from the question.

6 Some use of context.

Candidate Y, who is likely to achieve Grade 8, begins as follows:

1 Focuses on the question and supports with points about language from the outset.

2 Relates structure to tone.

3 Consistently comparative.

4 Compares the details of the language as well as the overarching themes.

5 Integrates appropriate terminology in a way that indicates it is being used to make a substantial point and not just for its own sake.

6 Begins to show a sense of alternative readings.

'Walking Away', like 'Mother, Any Distance', explores the tensions within a parent–child relationship as the child becomes increasingly independent. There is a more regretful tone to the former, as it is written by the parent who passively observes the child 'walking away', reflected in the repetition of the word 'away' in the title and then once in each stanza. In 'Mother', since the speaker is the child, he is the one who is moving forwards, so the movement away is described more positively. Enjambment stresses the word 'climb' by placing it at the end of line 9 and the word 'towards' by placing it at the beginning of line 14. Both suggest an advance by developing upwards or forwards. As a dramatic monologue, 'Mother' does not offer us the mother's perspective. When 'your fingertips still pinch / the last one-hundredth of an inch' there is a connotation of pain in the word 'pinch'. It is left ambiguous, however, whether she feels pain, because she is willing to suffer to let her child have the maximum freedom possible while still supporting him; or whether she inflicts pain on the son because she is unwilling to set him free. We do not see into her mind so we do not know. 'Walking' instead leaves us to infer the son's feelings and so focuses on the parent's sense of loss. The isolation of the father by the end of the poem is stressed by the final stanza beginning with the word 'I'.

Candidate X now continues:

Both poems use imagery to show changes in the relationships and the way the speaker feels about that. The first stanza of 'Mother' uses metaphors: 'the acres of the walls, the prairies of the floors.' These two images compare the inside of the new home to large outdoor areas; they show that the speaker feels tiny in comparison. When it talks about the tape measure we can see that the son wants more freedom but also is too scared to let go completely of the mother. The son has to report 'back to base'. Armitage uses alliteration to make it feel safe and comfortable. At the same time the 'b' sounds like marching, which can seem like he is too limited by rules. In the end it is the son who chooses to break this link: '...I reach'. The ellipsis shows he is stretching away. In 'Walking' the father starts by seeing the son as 'a satellite / Wrenched from its orbit'. This shows that the father thinks he ought to be the centre of the son's life. Later he is 'Like a winged seed loosened from its parent stem'. Parent plants need their offspring to grow away from them so that they don't need to share nutrients, which means this is good for the parent as well as the child. So both poems show the relationships with imagery.

1 Appropriate terminology used and effect of the technique identified.

2 Alternative interpretations suggested.

3 Again identifies effect.

4 Explains the ideas in the poem.

Candidate Y develops similar ideas at a more sophisticated level:

Both poems present a development in the feelings of the speaker towards the child's increasing independence, and both do so with imagery. In 'Walking' the speaker seems to come to terms with the idea that the child no longer needs him; in 'Mother' the narrator gradually becomes more adventurous about pushing boundaries. In 'Walking', the simile of 'like a satellite / Wrenched from its orbit' is frightening, since the natural place of a satellite is in orbit. Enjambment strengthens the sense of spiralling out of control.

1 Sustains and develops the comparison.

2 Relates ideas to both language and structure.

In the poet's life, Day Lewis' fear of losing his son in this way would be made worse by the fact that he started a new family with his second wife. By the third stanza this imagery has evolved via the 'half-fledged thing' of the second stanza to the simile of 'Like a winged seed loosened from its parent stem'. This feels more natural: partly this is an everyday image; and partly the meaning and the sound of the word 'loosened' are gentle, unlike the harsh 'wrenched' used previously. 'Mother' is similar because the choice to move further away lies with the child and not the parent.

3 Biographical context.

4 Highlights both similarities and differences.

Early on, Armitage uses 'the acres of the walls, the prairies of the floors.' This paradox of huge expanses of outdoor space being brought into his home conveys simultaneously his excitement in the newfound freedom of having his own home, and his vulnerability in seeming so small inside it. He therefore initially needs the tape measure to connect him to his mother. There is a double meaning for 'feeding'. Literally the tape is becoming longer, but metaphorically it is the umbilical cord feeding the child. We can see how supportive an image this presents of the mother by setting it within the context of other contemporary poets who have used the umbilical cord as a motif, such as the conflict fought with the daughter in Gillian Clarke's 'Catrin'. By the end of the poem he is able to let go of the tape measure in order to take the gamble that he will 'fall or fly'. The alliteration gives a sense of floating, so that he seems completely free of the mother. The sense of pushing boundaries is conveyed through placing these words within a short line in addition to the conventional fourteen lines of a sonnet. Thus both poems show the speaker becoming more willing to let go of the kind of parent–child relationship that had been appropriate when the child was younger. An important difference is that for the father in 'Walking' this causes sadness but for the child in 'Mother' it leads to excitement and adventure.

5 Literary context.

6 Expands by linking to form.

7 Finishes the paragraph by making an overall comparison relevant to the question that shows both similarities and differences.

Candidate X progresses:

> Both of the poems show the risks of children coping without their parents through the imagery of birds leaving the nest. In 'Walking' this is an upsetting image: 'the pathos of a half-fledged thing set free / Into a wilderness.' The bird is only half-fledged, which means it is being set free too early. The 'wilderness' shows that it is in danger. It uses enjambment, so it seems like being free is really falling off the end. The word 'pathos' shows that the father feels sorry for the child. In 'Mother', the bird imagery comes at the end of the poem, when the child has gained the most freedom. The speaker opens a 'hatch'. Although this is a noun that means an opening, 'hatch' can also be used as a verb for birds coming out of their shells. This is followed up with the language of 'fall or fly'. Whereas the speaker in 'Walking' sees only the risk of leaving the nest, in 'Mother' there is risk and excitement. Because 'fly' is the last word in the poem and because it rhymes with 'sky', I think that the speaker feels it is more likely that he will fly than fall.

1 Develops the comparison.

2 Relates structure and language to themes.

3 Offers a personal interpretation.

Candidate Y develops similar ideas:

> In each poem the imagery of birds leaving a nest is used to show the speaker's feelings about the child's ability to survive without the parent. In 'Walking' the focus is entirely on the danger this presents; whereas in 'Mother' there is an awareness of the risk but also of the benefits of taking a gamble. 'Walking' offers the disturbing image of 'the pathos of a half-fledged thing set free / Into a wilderness.' There is a sense that the child is moving towards maturity but not enough to survive without parental support, because he is only 'half-fledged'. The enjambment places the

1 Draws out similarities and differences.

word 'free' at the end of a line, so that it seems to fall into nothing; whereas 'wilderness' in the middle of the line gives a sense that the child will become hidden and so lost. In 'Mother' the imagery of flight comes instead at the climax, when the speaker opens a 'hatch'. Whereas in 'Walking', the half-fledged state represents a point along the child's development, in 'Mother' the hatching is a metaphor for the decision to break free. It is as if the son is reborn in this moment, achieving a fresh identity. Armitage uses assonance of the short vowel 'a' in 'a hatch that opens on an'. In one sense this feels empty, emphasising his fear at the lack of an external source of support, but it also suggests excited anticipation. This contrasts with the speaker's fear in 'Walking' that the 'half-fledged' bird cannot survive alone.

2 Explores effect of structure.

3 Examines language in detail.

4 Pulls the comparison together.

Candidate X concludes:

1 Selection of a relevant quotation, which could be improved by analysing the quote.

2 Identifies difference.

3 Uses relevant context.

The relationship with the mother in 'Mother' has been a springboard to enable the speaker now to survive without needing her. This is like the message of 'Walking' that 'selfhood begins with a walking away'. Both children need to let go of the parents to be themselves. In 'Walking' there is much more emphasis on this being a sacrifice for the parent. The ending of 'love is proved in the letting go' shows that the parent has had to let go even though he doesn't want to. We can relate this to Day Lewis calling the attention he got from his father after his mother died 'smother love'. In 'Mother' we are not given the opportunity to hear how the mother feels; instead the focus is on the need of the speaker to explore and take the risk of failure.

4 Does link the poems, but there is less on 'Mother, Any Distance' than on 'Walking Away'. The conclusion would feel more effective if more balanced.

Candidate Y concludes:

> A sense that the bond between parent and child is at once supremely close and yet depends upon knowing when to set the loved one free therefore fills both poems. In 'Mother', 'unreeling / years between us' is ambiguous. The mother has been supporting him for his entire life, so 'between' can mean that they have shared these years. However, in order for her to have provided this support, she must be of an older generation, so that the years form a barrier 'between' them. ◄——1 Considers alternative interpretations.
>
> This links to the use of enjambment from one stanza to another in 'Walking': 'go drifting away / Behind a scatter of boys.' The harsh-sounding 'b' alliteration here conveys the father's sense of chaos when these boys, symbolic of a different generation, intrude between parent and child. ◄—— The chief difference is that while 'Mother', from the child's perspective, shows positive progress, in 'Walking' there can only be reconciliation with a loss over which the parent has no control.

1 Considers alternative interpretations.

2 Again concisely blends points about structure and language with the focus on their effects. Technical language is not used for its own sake only, but to make a point that contributes to the argument.

Overall, Candidate X has achieved a strong Grade 5 through an engaged, comparative response that shows a clear understanding of the writers' use of language, form and structure. Candidate Y is working at the top end of Grade 8 and moving into Grade 9, with an informed personal response rooted in detailed attention to language, form and structure that focuses on the comparison throughout.

Sample responses for Section C – the Unseen

Below you will find examples of the type of questions you will see in Section C of your exam, followed by student responses to them.

First question

The first question here is on one poem: 'Blessing' by Imtiaz Dharker.

Blessing

The skin cracks like a pod.
There never is enough water.

Imagine the drip of it,
the small splash, echo
in a tin mug,
the voice of a kindly god.

Sometimes, the sudden rush
of fortune. The municipal pipe bursts,
silver crashes to the ground
and the flow has found
a roar of tongues. From the huts,
a congregation: every man woman
child for streets around
butts in, with pots,
brass, copper, aluminium,
plastic buckets,
frantic hands,

and naked children
screaming in the liquid sun,
their highlights polished to perfection,
flashing light,
as the blessing sings
over their small bones.

The question for this poem is:

In 'Blessing', how does the poet present feelings about water and the
lack of it?

(24 marks)

First let us look at the response of Candidate X, who is working around Grade 5:

> In 'Blessing' the poet describes people in a hot country who do not get enough water. We can tell because it is so hot that their skin actually cracks. The poem describes how on one occasion the people do get water and shows how excited they are. It starts by helping the reader to understand how it feels to go without water. The first stanza uses two end-stopped lines. This feels like nothing can flow. The onomatopoeia in 'cracks' helps it to sound dry and hard. It shows what it feels like when there is not enough water.

1 This is a structural point, but could be expressed more explicitly.

2 Now makes a clear point about the structure and goes on to identify the effect.

3 Blends this with a point about language and starts to explain the effect.

This is a promising start. Now let's take a look at how Candidate Y, who is working at Grade 8, tackles similar ideas:

> In 'Blessing' the poet tracks a succession of different feelings, beginning by encouraging the reader to empathise with the lack of water and progressing towards exploring how it feels for someone who usually has insufficient water suddenly to find themselves with an abundance of it. In the first stanza, the structure and language work together to give a sense of a barren world deprived of water. The end-stopping of both lines combines with the monosyllables of the first line to stop it from flowing. This reflects the failure of water to flow. The consonance of the hard 'k' sound in the simile 'The skin cracks like a pod', including the onomatopoeia of 'cracks', helps the reader to hear the way that everything is breaking up because of the lack of water.

1 There is more of a sense here that the poet is making deliberate structural choices and a focus on the effects.

2 Judiciously selects technical terms to make relevant points.

3 Develops this with detailed attention to language.

Candidate X now looks at how the first stanza contrasts with those that follow:

1 Technical terminology correctly used and effect identified.

2 Develops the consideration of effects.

> The poet makes the rest of the poem feel very different by using enjambment, so there is a feel of water flowing. An example is: 'rush / of fortune.' In the second stanza this comes from imagining the water, but in the rest of the poem it is because the water is actually there. The poem uses lots of soft sounds. A good example is 'small splash.' There is also onomatopoeia, meaning the reader can hear the sound of the water splashing. It helps the reader to understand how much the people in the poem want the water. When the people are trying to collect the water, there are lots of commas: 'butts in / with pots, / brass, copper, aluminium, / plastic buckets.' This helps to show that people are just using anything they can find to get the water. It also feels like it keeps stopping and starting, which is like the people bumping into each other as they try to get the water.

3 Considers more than one effect.

This is how Candidate Y develops similar points:

1 Candidate Y's strategy of stating the effect before the technique is a good way to avoid giving the impression of technique spotting.

> The second stanza invites the reader to imagine what it would feel like to have enough water. This is a clever way of making the reader empathise, because you would only need to imagine what having water feels like if you don't have it. The assonance in 'Imagine the drip of it' sounds like water dripping, so the poet is helping us to imagine by making us hear the sound of the water. This is followed by sibilance in 'small splash', which now sounds like rushing water. This stanza uses enjambment, which contrasts with the previous stanza to show the difference it makes when water is present because the poem now flows more. The enjambment and sibilance continue in the third stanza, for example in: 'Sometimes, the sudden rush / of

2 Picks up on the subtly different effects of two techniques.

89

3 Perceptive attention to the sounds of words.

fortune.' Once the people start to respond to the water, the poem uses plosives to convey the rush and the chaos: 'butts in, with pots, / brass, copper.' This helps us to understand the people's feelings because we can hear the way that they are crashing into each other in the excitement of trying to capture the water.

Candidate X's final paragraph is:

1 Well-selected quotation in support.

2 Begins to develop a personal response.

Lots of imagery in the poem links to religion. The poem is called 'Blessing' and the water is described using the metaphor of 'the voice of a kindly god.' It shows that the people worship the water. This can mean that even if the reader lives in a country where there is not a shortage of water it can help us understand how important water can be when you don't get enough. The children are 'naked' and they have 'small bones.' This shows that they are poor and so helps the reader feel sorry for them. It helps us understand how important it is that they get enough water.

The final part of Candidate Y's response is:

The poet also uses imagery to express how precious the people feel that water is. The whole poem is an extended metaphor. The title 'Blessing' has religious connotations. The water is personified in the second from last line because 'the blessing sings', which matches the metaphor 'The voice of a kindly god.' This feels like the water is something that people worship either as or like a god. The word 'congregation' could suggest the importance of water in many religious ceremonies, and also how it brings communities together. This shows how important people feel that water is in their lives. It could also suggest that they feel the lack of water is somehow a loss of god.

1 Considers alternative interpretations.

So the poem shows us how people feel when they lack water and then when they are surprised suddenly to find some. It also suggests the unfairness of this unequal distribution of water by using ambiguous language. The children in the final stanza are 'screaming' and have 'small bones.' They can be screaming with pleasure as they play in the water, but when they don't have enough water they would be screaming in pain. They have small bones because they are young, which feels sweet, but also because they are undernourished. So going without water symbolises them being deprived generally.

2 Develops by considering ambiguous language.

Second question

The second question asks for a comparison with 'Going for Water' by Robert Frost:

Going for Water

The well was dry beside the door,
And so we went with pail and can
Across the fields behind the house
To seek the brook if still it ran;

Not loth to have excuse to go,
Because the autumn eve was fair
(Though chill), because the fields were ours,
And by the brook our woods were there.

We ran as if to meet the moon
That slowly dawned behind the trees,
The barren boughs without the leaves,
Without the birds, without the breeze.

But once within the wood, we paused
Like gnomes that hid us from the moon,
Ready to run to hiding new
With laughter when she found us soon.

Each laid on other a staying hand
To listen ere we dared to look,
And in the hush we joined to make
We heard, we knew we heard the brook.

A note as from a single place,
A slender tinkling fall that made
Now drops that floated on the pool
Like pearls, and now a silver blade.

The second question, assessed on AO2 only, is:

Both 'Going for Water' and 'Blessing' describe the experience of needing water and then finding some. What are the similarities and/or differences between the ways the poets present this?

(8 marks)

Candidate X begins:

1 Focuses in on a technique in a comparative way.

2 Considers several effects.

In both poems there are similes and metaphors to explain what it feels like to need water and then to find some, for example comparing water and silver. In 'Blessing' it says 'silver crashes to the ground' and in 'Going for Water' it says the water is a 'silver blade'. This shows that water is really important because silver is a precious metal. It is also quite rare, which makes us think about how some people don't get enough water. These are effective images because flowing water can look like silver. In both poems this imagery is made to stand out because in 'Blessing' the word 'silver' is at the start of the line and in 'Going for Water' these are the last words of the poem. In 'Going for Water' it can also show that it is frightening because it is compared to a blade. This might be because of how it feels if you don't have water. Another difference is that in 'Blessing' — but not in 'Going for Water' — the water is also compared to a god.

3 Examines differences as well as similarities, but could go on to compare effects.

Candidate Y takes similar ideas, but develops them further:

> Both poems show how important finding water is through imagery, within which both compare water to silver. In 'Blessing' 'silver crashes to the ground', while 'Going for Water' closes with the image of the water as 'a silver blade'. In each case there is a sense of how valuable the water is. Silver has positive connotations of precious, natural and pure beauty, which are therefore transferred to the water. Yet in both poems there a sense of underlying menace. In 'Blessing' it seems inadequate by comparison with the extended religious metaphor. Also, silver has a sense of monetary value and there is a suggestion in the poem that it is economics rather than natural forces that deprive the people of water, because the 'municipal pipe' is always there but carrying water elsewhere. Enjambment is used so that 'silver' is the first word of the line immediately following the words 'the municipal pipe bursts'. So there is a disturbing sense that satisfying the human need for water can be dependent upon silver, in the sense of money. In 'Going for Water' the precious beauty of the water is emphasised by linking it to the image of the 'drops' being like 'pearls', as silver would be combined with pearls in decoration. Yet the final word of the poem is 'blade'. The pearls reflect the way that the poem shows childhood innocence through the search for water. Pearls look similar to the personified moon, with which the children play hide and seek: '<u>she</u> found us soon.' Just as 'Blessing' uses both positive and negative imagery, in 'Going for Water' discovering the water means the end of searching for it, which the characters had enjoyed.

1 Comparative, and focused on techniques and their effects.

2 Makes a similar point to Candidate X, but offers more detailed consideration and better use of technical terminology.

3 Compares both language and structure.

4 Links the comparison back to the question.

Candidate X finishes with:

1 Effects related to question.

'Blessing' uses an irregular structure. It does not rhyme and the stanzas and lines are different lengths. This reflects the way that the water is escaping from the pipe without control. It helps show how the people react with excitement and panic. The shortest stanza is the first one and the longest is third. This contrasts the time when the people don't have water but need it in stanza 1, with when there is more water than they can collect in stanza 3. In 'Going for Water' all the stanzas are four lines long and they have an ABCB rhyme scheme. This feels orderly and bouncy. It is like the excitement the speaker feels in playing a game while looking for the water and then in finding it. The rhyme can help to link the speaker with the water. In the fifth stanza 'look' rhymes with 'brook'. This joins the action of the people looking for water to the brook that contains the water. This is like the way that in 'Blessing', when the water is spraying everywhere, the people are also in chaos.

2 Compares structure.

3 Brief, relevant quotations.

Candidate Y concludes:

1 Links comparisons to effects.

2 Notices regular rhythm.

Both poems use the structure to encourage empathy with the characters who are seeking water, and both do so by creating a pattern that is then disrupted. The regular stanza length, iambic tetrameter and regular ABCB rhyme scheme of 'Going for Water' all help to convey the childlike purity of the search for water, by seeming neat and purposeful. By contrast, 'Blessing' uses irregular stanza and line lengths and avoids end rhyme. The poet uses the irregularity to help the reader understand how it feels suddenly to have water. The water begins to flow not only in the imagination but also in reality in the third stanza. Because this is the longest stanza of the poem and because there is enjambment not only within the stanza but also between stanzas 3 and 4, there is a sense in which the flow of the water causes the flow of the excitement in the people. Although the poem generally does not rhyme, lines 9 and 10 rhyme with 'ground' and 'found'. This is the point when the water connects with the people, so the sudden use of rhyme gives a sense of things working in a way not normally possible in this society.

3 Close attention to detail.

Both candidates have managed to find interesting points within the constraints of an Unseen exam question. You should be able to see that overall Candidate Y makes more effective use of technical vocabulary than Candidate X, develops points in more detail, and is more sensitive to alternative readings.

1 'When We Two Parted':

In secret we met—
In silence I grieve

(ll. 25–26)

- In the first line of the quote the pronoun used is 'we' but in the second it is 'I'. The word 'we' is emphasised by the assonance of 'secret we' and 'grieve'; 'I' is stressed by the assonance of 'silence I'. The 'we' refers to them as a couple; the 'I' refers to the speaker after the break-up, suggesting his feeling of abandonment.

2 'Love's Philosophy':

And the sunlight clasps the earth,
And the moonbeams kiss the sea

(ll. 13–14)

- This is useful as an example of sublime, natural imagery. In many cultures the sun is presented as masculine and the moon as feminine. So this can help the speaker to argue that nature favours romantic relationships between men and women.

3 'Porphyria's Lover':

at last I knew
Porphyria worshipped me;

(ll. 32–33)

- The word 'knew' suggests the speaker's arrogance, which is emphasised by the enjambment in these lines.

4 Sonnet 29 – 'I think of thee!':

I will not have my thoughts instead of thee

(l. 6)

- The line starts with 'I' and ends with 'thee'. The word 'thoughts' comes between them. This could show that the thoughts, instead of uniting the couple, are threatening to divide them.

'Neutral Tones':

And the sun was white, as though chidden of God,

(l. 2)

5

- This is a compact example of the poem's use of colour, religious ideas and predominantly monosyllabic vocabulary. You could therefore use it to illustrate many of the ideas discussed in the commentary (see pp. 19–21).

'Letters from Yorkshire':

Is your life more real because you dig and sow?

(l. 9)

6

- Prior to this question the focus is on what separates the two characters; afterwards it shifts to what unites them. This question therefore forms a pivotal moment in the poem.

'The Farmer's Bride':

The short days shorten and the oaks are brown,

(l. 34)

7

- Seasons and colours are used throughout the poem to show how the narrator sees the world, for instance the 'brown' here could mean he is allying the bride with the earth. The use of the colour brown is also important because when the farmer is starting to lose control he describes the bride with 'the brown, / The brown of her'.

'Walking Away':

I can see
You walking away from me

(ll. 6–7)

8

- The enjambment placed on the word 'see' draws attention to the fact that the reader is seeing through the speaker's eyes but isn't given the child's point of view. The pronouns 'I' and 'You' are on separate lines, which reveals the speaker's feeling of the child being separated from him.

9

'Eden Rock':

The sky whitens as if lit by three suns.

(l. 13)

- In the poem light and white are used to symbolise purity, perfection and truth. They are united in this image.

10

'Follower':

I wanted to grow up and plough,

(l. 17)

- This encapsulates the child's longing to become like the father and so relates to the theme of 'following'.

11

'Mother, Any Distance':

to breaking point, where something
has to give;

(ll. 10–11)

- The enjambment indicates that the narrator is pushing beyond boundaries. The three-syllable line is suddenly much shorter than all the previous lines. This relates to the idea of recreating the rules. The narrator can also be expressing a feeling of excitement at the possibilities that this opens up. The empty space this leaves at the end of the line also suggests a sense of loss – a fear at continuing without the mother's support.

12

'Before You Were Mine':

your ghost clatters towards me

(l. 13)

- The onomatopoeia helps to make this image more vivid. The mother is described as 'your ghost', however, as if this past self has died and cannot be regained except in the imagination or memory.

'Winter Swans':

like a pair of wings settling after flight.

(l. 20)

13

- This final line draws the swan imagery together and focuses it on the couple's reconciliation.

'Singh Song!':

vee cum down whispering stairs

(l. 46)

14

- Personifying the stairs, so that they are 'whispering', suggests that really it is the couple who are whispering. This could give a sense of childish enjoyment, or of intimacy between the couple. It might alternatively indicate that they have no privacy, because even once the shop is shut they need to whisper so that they cannot be overheard. This line also exemplifies well the non-standard spelling and grammar.

'Climbing My Grandfather':

the wrinkles well-spaced
and easy

(ll. 21–22)

15

- The 'wrinkles', which some might see as undesirable, are presented as attractive to the climbing grandchild. It helps to show the love for the grandfather and the intimacy of their relationship.

Practice questions for the Unseen poetry section

Below are examples of pairs of poems on a range of themes, as well as sample questions that are broadly similar to those you might be set in the examination. Do remember, though, that the Unseen questions can be on any theme at all. Have a read through these questions and have a go at answering some of them in a timed practice. Most of these poems can be found fairly easily on the internet.

Love

'First Love' by John Clare (*Selected Poems*, Faber and Faber)

'A Broken Appointment' by Thomas Hardy (*Collected Poems*, Wordsworth)

1 In 'First Love', how does the speaker present his feelings about falling in love?
2 In 'First Love' and 'A Broken Appointment' the speakers write about the presence or absence of a loved person. What are the similarities and/ or differences in the way this is described?

Parents and children

'For a Five-Year-Old' by Fleur Adcock (*Selected Poems*, Oxford University Press)

'Looking for Dad' by Brian Patten (*Gargling With Jelly*, Viking Kestrel)

1 How does the speaker in 'For a Five-Year-Old' present the way parents relate to children?
2 Both 'For a Five-Year-Old' and 'Looking for Dad' present differences between the viewpoints of adults and children. What are the similarities and/or differences in the ways they present this?

Growing up

'Blackberry-Picking' by Seamus Heaney (*Death of a Naturalist*, Faber and Faber)

'In Mrs Tilscher's Class' by Carol Ann Duffy (*The Other Country*, Anvil Press)

1 In 'Blackberry-Picking', how does the poet present the experiences of picking blackberries?
2 Both 'Blackberry-Picking' and 'In Mrs Tilscher's Class' present the loss of childhood innocence. What are the similarities and/or differences in the ways the poets present this?

Loss of a loved one

'Stop All the Clocks' by W.H. Auden (*Collected Poems*, Faber and Faber)

'Do Not Go Gentle into that Good Night' by Dylan Thomas (*Collected Poems*, Weidenfeld and Nicolson)

1 In 'Stop All the Clocks', how does the speaker present the ways people are affected by the loss of a loved one?

2 Both 'Stop All the Clocks' and 'Do Not Go Gentle into that Good Night' express feelings about losing a loved one. What are the similarities and/or differences between the ways the poets present these feelings?

alliteration: the repetition of the same sound at the beginning of words

assonance: the repetition of a vowel sound

caesura: a break or pause in a line of poetry

consonance: the repetition of similar-sounding consonants

dramatic monologue: a poem written as the speech of a single character

end-stopping: using punctuation at the end of a line

enjambment: where the sentence or clause runs over on to the next line

free verse: poetry that does not rhyme or have a regular rhythm

half rhyme: where words have similar, but not identical, sounds

iamb: a unit of two beats, the first unstressed and the second stressed

- **iambic tetrameter:** four iambs to a line
- **iambic pentameter:** five iambs to a line

metaphor: using one thing to represent another, saying 'X *is* Y'

octet: a unit of eight lines

pathetic fallacy: using background details, such as the weather or landscape, to tell the reader about the emotional state of a character, often by attributing the character's feelings to the background

personification: the attribution of human feelings to objects or animals

Petrarchan sonnet: a type of sonnet that uses the rhyme scheme to divide the fourteen lines into an octet and a sestet (see also entry for 'sonnet')

plosives: hard, explosive sounds like *t, d, p, b, k, g*

quatrain: a unit of four lines

sestet: a unit of six lines

sibilance: repetition of hissing or buzzing sounds like *s, sh, z*

simile: comparing two things, saying 'X *is like* Y'

sonnet: a fourteen-line poem, usually in iambic pentameter

stanza: a group of lines; a verse

syntax: the ordering of words in a sentence

Below are listed suitable comparative poems for each of the poems in the 'Love and Relationships' cluster.

- 'When We Two Parted': 'She Walks in Beauty' by Lord Byron
- 'Love's Philosophy': 'To a Skylark' by Percy Bysshe Shelley
- 'Porphyria's Lover': 'St Simeon Stylites' by Lord Tennyson
- Sonnet 29 'I think of thee!': Sonnet 43 'How do I love thee?' by Elizabeth Barrett Browning
- 'Neutral Tones': 'Nobody Comes' by Thomas Hardy
- 'The Farmer's Bride': 'No Buyers: a Street Scene' by Thomas Hardy
- 'Walking Away': 'The House Where I Was Born' by Cecil Day Lewis
- 'Letters from Yorkshire': 'The Thought-Fox' by Ted Hughes
- 'Eden Rock': 'To My Father' by Charles Causley
- 'Follower': 'Digging' by Seamus Heaney
- 'Mother, Any Distance': 'Kid' by Simon Armitage
- 'Before You Were Mine': 'Brothers' by Carol Ann Duffy
- 'Winter Swans': 'Farther' by Owen Sheers
- 'Singh Song!': 'Parade's End' by Daljit Nagra
- 'Climbing My Grandfather': 'Looking for the Comet' by Andrew Waterhouse

Answers to the 'Review your learning' sections.

Poem-by-poem commentaries

1 Byron and Shelley.
2 Robert Browning and Elizabeth Barrett Browning.
3 'Follower'.
4 Carol Ann Duffy.
5 a Wales.   b 'Winter Swans'.
6 'Mother, Any Distance'.

Themes

1 'Singh Song!' and Sonnet 29 – 'I think of thee!'
2 'Porphyria's Lover' and 'The Farmer's Bride'.
3 'Walking Away'.
4 'Climbing My Grandfather'.
5 Any from: criticism, disrespect, rebellion, mockery.

Assessment Objectives and skills

1 The ability to read, understand and respond to the text.
2 Writers' methods: language, form and structure.
3 Understanding the relationships between texts and their contexts.
4 AO1, AO2 and AO3.
5 AO1 and AO2.
6 AO2.

Tackling the exams (Section B)

1 Two.
2 Yes.
3 'Compare'.
4 Revise the poems comparatively.
5 Technique spotting is when a student identifies a method without explaining the effect created by it. This will not gain many marks.

Tackling the exams (Section C)

1 Two.   2 One.   3 Two.
4 You cannot grasp the full meaning of a poem if you read it only once.
5 Without planning, you may end up contradicting and/or repeating yourself.